DISCARD

RESEARCH AND DEVELOPMENT
AND SCHOOL CHANGE

A Symposium of
THE LEARNING RESEARCH AND DEVELOPMENT CENTER
UNIVERSITY OF PITTSBURGH
Robert Glaser and William Cooley, Chairmen

RESEARCH AND DEVELOPMENT AND SCHOOL CHANGE

Edited by ROBERT GLASER

Contributors

Benjamin S. Bloom   Wayne H. Holtzman
Joseph M. Cronin   Wesley W. Posvar
Robert M. Gagné   Alberta E. Siegel
Jacob W. Getzels   Ralph W. Tyler

 LAWRENCE ERLBAUM ASSOCIATES, PUBLISHERS
1978   Hillsdale, New Jersey

DISTRIBUTED BY THE HALSTED PRESS DIVISION OF
JOHN WILEY & SONS
New York   Toronto   London   Sydney

Lawrence Erlbaum Associates, Inc., Publishers
62 Maria Drive
Hillsdale, New Jersey 07642

Distributed solely by Halsted Press Division
John Wiley & Sons, Inc., New York

Library of Congress Cataloging in Publication Data

Main entry under title:

Research and development and school change

   1. Educational research—United States—Congresses.
I. Glaser, Robert, 1921– II. Pittsburgh. Univer-
sity. Learning Research and Development Center.
LB1028.R338   370′.78′073   78-8914
ISBN 0-470-26415-2

Printed in the United States of America

TABLE OF CONTENTS

PREFACE

The essays included in this book are based on papers presented at a symposium held in March 1976 at the Learning Research and Development Center (LRDC), University of Pittsburgh. The symposium was planned to serve three purposes: first, to pay tribute to Ralph W. Tyler, retiring chairman of LRDC's Board of Visitors; second, to mark the dedication of LRDC's new building; and third, to provide an opportunity for those of us involved in educational research and development to reflect further on its implications for school change.

At the time the Center was established in the early 1960s, there was a virtual absence of research organizations working on the interaction between educational practice and scientific knowledge. In fields other than education, professional pressures appeared to stimulate basic research and, in turn, basic research findings were applied in the development of new technologies. For educational practice, however, there were no national institutes and few research and development laboratories.

One part of the problem was the lack of recognized status and favorable working environments for scientists interested in problems of applied human learning or in the analysis and management of instructional processes. For instance, experimental psychology was not hospitable to questions arising from instructional practice; experimental researchers who had not already gained prominence in the laboratory could not afford to turn their attention to problems of educational practice.

Another part of the problem was that schools of education and behavioral science departments, even at the same university, lived in different worlds and seldom interacted. As a result, most studies done on teaching methodology made little contact with data and theory from the behavioral sciences. While such studies helped with immediate practical decisions, they contributed much less to building an organized body of knowledge that could contribute to the long-range improvement of instruction.

One solution to this problem was to provide special settings that would foster interaction between the behavioral and social sciences and educational practice. Organizations were needed that afforded the climate and the facilities for maximizing research directed toward educationally relevant areas—research that was both highly fundamental in character and, at the same time, directed toward practical problems in education.

Today, the situation has changed. Educational research and development programs, university centers, and regional laboratories have been established. There is a growing demand among educational administrators, teachers, and state departments of education for analytical and evaluative research on school problems. And, there is increased attention by behavioral and social scientists to research areas relevant to individual learning, teaching materials and practices, and the design of classroom environments. The major problem of today is to establish focused priorities for work that can be carried out by highly qualified individuals who are aware of available scientific and professional resources and social needs.

In this context, the contributors to this volume raise such questions as the following: What has resulted from the increase in educational research and development activity? How has it effected school change? These general questions are discussed from a variety of perspectives in the essays that follow. Issues are raised that are important to consider in future efforts directed toward improving education.

Wesley Posvar, in the opening essay, discusses the concept of the university research center and how it should be defined, organized, and supported. He examines the interdisciplinary approach and defines some important principles that should underlie the formation of effective research and development organizations in a university setting.

Wayne Holtzman follows with a review of the expansion of federal involvement in American education and relates this expansion to the changing character of society. He concludes with an analysis of some of the problems that face research and development in education for the future.

Joseph Cronin, Superintendent of the Illinois Office of Education, provides another perspective on the role of research and development in educational change and also leaves us with some challenging problems for the future, He discusses the kind of research that is needed by educational decision makers and how the conduct of educational research and development might be changed in order to more effectively impact the schools.

Jacob Getzels, in the next essay, demonstrates how theoretical research has been instrumental in school change since the beginning of the 20th century. He cites theoretical studies that have affected education in three areas—curriculum and instruction, educational policy, and the preparation of educational practitioners.

Alberta Siegel also discusses the role of basic research in social change. Her focus is on research in child development and its relevance for designing social institutions. She covers a broad spectrum of research on children and young adults and relates it to a variety of institutions, including the family, day care centers, and schools.

Benjamin Bloom examines how educational evaluation can and has contributed to the improvement of education. Much has been learned over the past 20 years about how to evaluate instruction and learning and how the evaluation process can be integrally related to educational objectives. His chapter provides a review of this rapidly developing field and insight into some of the directions it will take in the future.

Robert Gagné pulls together many of the issues raised by the other authors. He discusses trends and accomplishments in research, in the development of educational products and procedures, in the field of evaluation, and in dissemination since a national research and development program was established. He lists some substantial accomplishments, and, as many of the other authors, things yet to be done.

The concluding essay by Ralph Tyler draws on his years of experience and range of involvement in education. He describes how the results of research and development are currently employed by the schools and discusses the role each participant plays—researchers, developers, school practitioners, teacher-training institutions, educational publishers, and state departments of education. Throughout his essay, he offers suggestions for transmitting the results of research and development to the schools.

Taken together, these essays are a fitting collection for the occasion of this dedication volume. They serve as a strong reminder that educational research and development must combine a commitment to the continued improvement of our schools with new developments in scientific knowledge and careful study of school practices.

As Chairmen of the symposium, we would like to thank the many individuals who contributed to the preparation of this book. We are particularly grateful to LRDC's Board of Visitors for their contributions and for the counsel they have provided to LRDC over the years. We would also like to thank William Rea, Wesley Posvar, and Rhoten Smith of the University of Pittsburgh for their continued support and understanding of research institutes such as LRDC.

Robert Glaser
William W. Cooley

RALPH W. TYLER's distinguished career in education is marked by scholarship, diversity, and social impact. After graduating from Doane College in 1921, he taught high school in Pierre, South Dakota. In 1927, he received his Ph.D from the University of Chicago and from 1928 to 1953 served there as Chairman of the Department of Education, as University Examiner, and as Dean of the Division of Social Sciences. He has also served on the faculties of the universities of Nebraska and North Carolina and of Ohio State University.

While at Chicago, Dr. Tyler became nationally known for his direction of the Eight-Year Study, a classic in the empirical investigation of the relationships of teaching methods to the outcomes of education. The methods of appraisal of learning outcomes developed in this study were an important landmark in educational research.

In 1953, Dr. Tyler founded the Center for Advanced Study in the Behavioral Sciences, an institution he directed for 15 years. He currently is Director Emeritus of the Center and Senior Consultant with Science Research Associates. In 1965, he became the first president of the National Academy of Education, which was established to support scholarship in education. During the course of his work, Dr. Tyler has been the recipient of numerous awards for distinguished teaching, contributions to educational policy, and for research.

This very brief summary only begins to relate the many working and advisory capacities by which Ralph Tyler has influenced educational thought and action. The governmental commissions and educational organizations that have been guided by his counsel are too numerous to list and his willingness to be of service to others is documented by thousands of miles of travel.

As Chairman of the LRDC Board of Visitors between 1964 and 1975, he has been a singularly important figure in its history. He has guided LRDC in its development through his insistence that the challenge of providing quality education to all is still unfinished business, through his ability to be both constructively critical and strongly supportive, and through his unique understanding of the complexities of the relationships between scientific research, educational practice, and social change.

LRDC was established in 1963 by a group of behavioral scientists and educators who were concerned about the relationship between educational research and practice. Their goal was to design an organization in which sustained and programmatic research would be fostered that would contribute to the understanding of learning and the improvement of educational practice. In 1964, the Center was designated by the Cooperative Research Branch of the U. S. Office of Education as one of the first university-based research and development centers, and in 1971 was one of four research and development organizations awarded a grant by USOE for the construction of permanent facilities.

The staff of LRDC consists of individuals from different disciplines and professions: psychologists from a variety of fields, evaluation researchers, curriculum designers, and educational supervisors and implementers, many of whom are experienced classroom teachers and school administrators. Sociologists, experimental design experts, and computer scientists further reflect the Center's diversity of talents. These individuals conduct research in a number of areas important to education: learning and cognition as it relates to instruction, the design of improved instructional practices and classroom processes, the development of evaluation and implementation methodology, and assessment of the effectiveness of school programs.

The Center's new building provides the many settings required for research and development in education, containing laboratories for basic research, facilities for field research and instructional design, and demonstration classrooms. LRDC has adopted a mode of operation in which there is a close interaction between research and practice. Cognitive and social processes are studied both in the laboratories and in school settings. Instructional procedures and materials and evaluation methodology are given pilot tryout in associated schools before more extensive application. In all its work, the Center strives to contribute to both the art and science of teaching and learning.

The work of the Center has been supported by many organizations: by long-range support from the National Institute of Education and the University of Pittsburgh, and by numerous governmental agencies and private foundations and corporations, including the Baldwin-Whitehall School District, Buhl Foundation, Carnegie Foundation, Ford Foundation, New Century Publishing Company, General Learning Corporation, Hillman Foundation, Imperial International Learning Corporation, Jack and Jill Foundation, Model Cities, National Science Foundation, Pittsburgh Board of Education, Pennsylvania Department of Education, Office of Naval Research, U. S. Office of Education, Westinghouse Corporation, and the Wilkinsburg School District.

LRDC BOARD OF VISITORS
1964-1977

LRDC RESEARCH ASSOCIATES

James Algina
Center Associate
Assistant Professor of Education

Isabel Beck
Assistant Professor of Education

William Bickel
Research Assistant Professor of Education

Karen Block
Associate Professor of Education

John Bolvin
Professor of Education

Lloyd Bond
Assistant Professor of Psychology

M. Elizabeth Boston
Research Associate

Audrey Champagne
Research Associate Professor of Education

Michelene Chi
Research Assistant Professor of Psychology

William Cooley
Professor of Education

Roy Creek
Assistant Professor of Education

R. Tony Eichelberger
Assistant Professor of Education

Evelyn Fisher
Lecturer, Sociology

Irene Frieze
Assistant Professor of Psychology

Robert Glaser, Co-Director
University Professor of Psychology and
    Education

Doris Gow
Research Assistant Professor of Education

James Greeno
Professor of Psychology

J. Ernest Harrison
Research Associate

Burkart Holzner
Professor of Sociology

James J. Kelly, Jr.
Center Associate
Dean, School of Education

Leopold Klopfer
Professor of Education

Gaea Leinhardt
Research Assistant Professor of
    Psychology

Alan Lesgold
Assistant Professor of Psychology

John Levine
Associate Professor of Psychology

C. Mauritz Lindvall
Professor of Education

Don Lyon
Post-Doctoral Fellow

James Pellegrino
Assistant Professor of Psychology

Charles Perfetti
Associate Professor of Psychology

Lauren Resnick, Co-Director
Professor of Psychology and of Education

Warren Shepler
Professor of Education

Alexander Siegel
Professor of Psychology

James Voss
Professor of Psychology

Margaret Wang
Research Associate Professor of Education

Naomi Zigmond
Associate Professor of Education

THE UNIVERSITY AND THE RESEARCH CENTER

WESLEY W. POSVAR
Chancellor
University of Pittsburgh

As a preface to this symposium, I would like to remark generally about the larger context of the university research center as a new type of organization—its development, its functions, its problems, and its prospects. First, let us think a moment about the very idea of research. Only during the past century did research on a large scale come to be regarded as an essential adjunct of modern civilization, an activity that is capable of enriching it and also, more recently, of tackling its pressing technological and social problems. Only in the latter half of this century, stimulated by the awesome results of concentrated research during World War II, did research become organized, directed, and focused upon major tasks and goals. In our common usage, this phase is called research and development, or R&D, and it is an item that looms large in the budgets of governments and corporations. In the past 20 years, government and industry in the United States increased their annual expenditures on R&D from $6 billion to $35 billion. A small fraction of this amount, now about $3 billion, is expended in universities, and of that, about $2 billion is from federal funds.

While the lion's share of research funds is expended in highly organized government and corporate laboratories, I like to think that the university research activity is the heart of the whole effort; this is due to autonomy of university faculties and the spirit of creativity that does or ought to flourish in a university environment. On the campus, we can be more critical of existing ways of doing things and more bold about testing new avenues and assumptions.

We can also deal in a longer time period. It is estimated that corporate laboratories have a horizon of one to two years, and

1

government laboratories must look to at least visible goals; however, universities can look beyond the horizon. At a recent meeting of advisers to the U. S. Energy Research Development Administration, I made the strong point that university research must be nourished along with the vast organized laboratories for the simple reason that we have a capability and potential in this area that are unique.

Let me now relate the idea of research to the mission of the university itself. We are accustomed to thinking of teaching and research as a mutually reinforcing set of tasks. Conscious as we are of our medieval academic origins and regalia, we may not be fully aware that the research function has been elaborated only in modern times. In the late 19th century, research developed along with and partly as a result of the rise of the academic department. The department was and is based upon the principle that related subject matter and investigative methods should be grouped together by what we call the "academic discipline." Within the department, the discipline associates scholars of like training and interests. The discipline has proved to be a remarkably creative force; witness the achievements of individuals working together under the banner of physics, of chemistry, of physiology, or of political economy. When the investigations of these people accelerated and became more and more sophisticated, many subgroupings were spawned as full-bodied disciplines, such as nuclear physics, astrophysics, biochemistry, molecular biology, political science, economics, and sociology. At the University of Pittsburgh alone, we have 110 academic departments that are devoted to about 100 different academic disciplines.

In the last 30 years, another dramatic advance has been made in research organization and method. As intellectual investigation greatly increased, there appeared the need for kinds of activity that cut across disciplines, following what is called the interdisciplinary or multidisciplinary approach. This approach soon took on organizational form.

The interdisciplinary approach is embodied in the university research center, which characteristically is staffed by people from a variety of disciplines who share an interest in a particular class of problems. The interdisciplinary idea is also put into practice in somewhat more structured nonuniversity laboratories, and also in the independent "think tanks," some of which resemble university centers. The concept of organizing the efforts of people with different skills and backgrounds soon led to investigative activities called "systems analysis." It has many meanings, but it entails defining and examining a problem area seen as a "system," with components, boundaries, and interacting parts and causal relationships.

The development of interdisciplinary centers is sometimes seen as a way to supersede academic departments, or to avoid their limitations in terms of orthodoxy and compartmentalization. These may indeed be drawbacks, but I think the interdisciplinary movement is an exciting adjunct to, not a replacement for, the academic disciplines. The concept of the center and of systematic or interdisciplinary analysis should not deny the importance of the disciplines, for it usually depends and is built upon the disciplines of the individual investigators. Moreover, the center represents an alternative, but not more important, strategy for mobilizing intellectual expertise. There are exciting sets of problems amenable to solution by physicists with a more narrow range of interests, and other sets of problems that are amenable to selected groups of scientists of different disciplines. The Learning Research and Development Center (LRDC) at the University of Pittsburgh, for example, is concerned with the set of problems associated with the human learning process, and its staff includes cognitive, developmental, and social psychologists, sociologists, anthropologists, educational designers and evaluators, and computer scientists.

While I think that the interdisciplinary development is vital and exciting, it is also immature. Within the University, the existence of centers leads to what we call a matrix organization which has some difficulties. In a matrix organization, there is the usual hierarchy of faculties of departments and schools in which responsibilities are arranged vertically. There are also individuals from the different departments and schools gathered together in the centers, which are, thus, horizontal slices across the institution. Most of the members of centers, therefore, sit in two boxes of an organizational chart, the center plus the home academic

3

department. This can result in ambiguities of budgetary control and accountability. The academic department may have a weak relationship with those members who are physically absent and whose main work is in the center, while the directors of centers may feel that their members' attentions are tugged away by their departments. There is no simple place to put centers on the organizational chart, so they tend as a group to report to a chief academic officer, a provost, or a vice president, often creating problems of span of control.

Centers also do not always represent the best mobilization of the universities' inner resources of talent. Institutional tensions—jealousies or conflicts between centers and departments—can result when resources and skills are uncoordinated or duplicated. Centers are often not related enough to the academic community, and sometimes are flawed in their capacity for neutral and objective analysis.

There is also a set of problems stemming from the relationship of research centers with clients. A center may be inclined to set its premises to meet the expectations of the client, whether deliberately or not. In some cases the sponsoring agency may subtly suggest, or in more obvious ways indicate that the outcome should be supportive of its own point of view. Centers may—and this is a particular danger—fall to the temptations of entrepreneurship, and seek expanding scale and funds as a measure of satisfaction and success in itself. In some universities, centers have proliferated too much because they grew in response to funding sources that were easy to accept. There is one campus reporting over 150 centers. Actually, a good many of them are not research centers in the sense in which I have defined them.

A related concern is that compared with traditional academic research, there is a tendency for research centers to focus their energies on studies that can lead to ready applications of investigative results to problems defined outside the center. I think that this tendency is not inherent, but follows from the greater availability of funds for the support of studies that have definable outcomes. The center idea can be just as potent, in my view, in basic scientific work and in work that has no sharply prescribed or expected outcome.

Because the university research center does represent a still-emerging concept, and because of these pitfalls, I have certain informal ground rules about how they should be defined, organized, and supported. First, the center should be truly interdisciplinary or interschool in its character and its membership; it should be in fact a center, not a tangential or dissociated activity. It should be a system, the sum greater than its parts, and should bring together people who draw upon their disciplines and relate to them, not be insulated from them. I think the centers at the University of Pittsburgh meet this test very well; along with LRDC, there is the Center for International Studies, the Knowledge Availability Systems Center, the Space Research Coordination Center, the Philosophy of Science Center, and some others. There are many instances in higher education, however, of a center's being used as an insulating shield or a diversion, in which case the center can be more a liability than an asset to the parent institution.

The center's mission and goals should be defined, and they should be reexamined at intervals. Without this process, there is lack of coherence and organizing purpose, and a too-easy tendency for proliferation and entrepreneurship. Its central activity must be research, and training should be subsidiary. A center should not enter into a "brokerage" activity whereby it accepts funds solely to hire outsiders to do a job; the center should be a part of the university, and it should bring educational benefits back to the institution. Finally, the center should represent an efficient and meaningful assembly of the university's resources, consistent with the priorities of the institution. The centers I just mentioned meet this test. One area, however, in which the University's resources are intriguingly powerful and are not yet fully mobilized and focused for interdisciplinary research is that which includes the life sciences, biological sciences, chemical sciences, and the basic sciences of medicine and the other health schools.

In all of our research activities within a university, whether conducted by departments or centers, there is a persisting dilemma or even tension between the idea of directed or organized research and that of undirected research—that which follows the particular interests of the investigator. I think that research activity is needed along the whole spectrum from what is called directed and undirected, and this is true both within disciplines and within centers. The question, really, is who does the directing. It is worth noting that the Salk vaccine discovery at the University of Pittsburgh resulted from a highly organized investigative activity. The interests of several of our faculty in new sources of energy are at this stage quite undirected. I submit that when these professors are ready to launch a major effort they will carefully organize their energies and their use of resources.

In conclusion, let me say that research centers, such as the Learning Research and Development Center, are a very important element of this University. They represent a new organizing principle for intellectual investigation. It is one that makes universities more important institutions than ever and one that gives promise of great benefit to society.

SOCIAL CHANGE
AND
THE RESEARCH AND DEVELOPMENT
MOVEMENT

WAYNE H. HOLTZMAN
President, Hogg Foundation for Mental Health
Professor of Psychology and Education, University of Texas

The most notable characteristic of modern research and development in American education is the incredible expansion of federal involvement in the 1960s, followed by the sharp retrenchment of the 1970s. Major social changes in American society parallel this expansion and contraction. A closer examination of these social changes sheds insight upon what has happened to the research and development movement in education. But before examining current American society and the contemporary research and development movement, let us review some of the highlights of the past century.

The first federal involvement in education began under the first President Johnson over 100 years ago. On March 11, 1867, Dr. Henry Barnard was appointed the first Commissioner of Education by President Andrew Johnson. Congress charged this new department with a research and development mission of obtaining statistics and facts that would show national progress in education. This passive policy of reflecting the current state of affairs by publishing educational statistics remained in force for 87 years until the passage of the Cooperative Research Act in 1954, marking the beginning of the modern era. Throughout this period, the major thrust of ideas for research and development in education grew out of the great private universities and their experimental school projects. Consisting initially of philosophical inquiries and debates, pedagogy evolved at the turn of the century into a psychologically based empiricism and a new science of education. The intellectual roots of modern research and development can be traced most clearly through one university and its influence, the University of Chicago.

In the first half of this century, three great leaders of educational research set the pace at the University of Chicago. First came John Dewey in 1894 as chairman of philosophy, psychology, and pedagogy. The establishment of a laboratory school emphasized the functional relationship between school learning and real life experiences. From 1904 until 1938, Charles Hubbard Judd held forth as chairman of the Department of Education. The science of education and the pyschology of reading owe much to his leadership.

Among Judd's young graduate students in the 1920s was Ralph W. Tyler, who later served as research associate, university examiner, and chairman of education succeeding Judd in 1938. As director of the university's Bureau of Educational Research, Tyler undertook the eight-year school curriculum study which has had a profound influence upon American education that is still strongly in evidence today. The construction of achievement tests, the appraisal and recording of student progress, the development of basic principles for curriculum and instruction, the precise specification of instructional objectives, the careful design of instructional sequences, and the empirical evaluation of the outcome of such instruction constitute a comprehensive syllabus for education. Tyler's successor, Francis Chase, continued to carry on in the Chicago tradition. His 1972 report on the Regional Educational Laboratory Program points out how these major intellectual roots are tied together.

The Learning Research and Development Center (LRDC) at the University of Pittsburgh can be seen as the confluence of these three main influences growing out of the University of Chicago—John Dewey with his progressive education and laboratory schools, Charles Judd who championed functional psychology and experimental research, and Ralph Tyler who emphasized comprehensive integration of these other ideas with evaluation of changes in behavior and a school curriculum designed to meet specific objectives. LRDC is the reality of these influences merged successfully into one research and development program.

THE PITTSBURGH LEARNING RESEARCH
AND DEVELOPMENT CENTER

As Salmon-Cox and Holzner (1976) point out in their analysis of LRDC as an organization, a grant to the University of Pittsburgh from the Buhl Foundation in 1963 brought together Robert Glaser and Steele Gow as co-directors of a new program. This unique combination of Glaser, with his advanced research on programmed instruction and criterion-referenced testing, and Gow, the political scientist, who was then serving as director of the university's Coordinated Education Center, provided just the right chemistry for rapid development. The Learning Research and Development Center was formed the next year and was funded under the Cooperative Research Act as one of the first of the new federally sponsored research and development centers. The idea of a new role for researcher-developer was quickly established in the new Individually Prescribed Instruction (IPI) Project at Oakleaf Elementary School. By 1968, an interaction model had been established at Frick School in the Primary Education Project, where professionals were involved in multiple roles ranging from basic research to developmental engineering. By 1970, three major programs had evolved—instructional design and evaluation, learning research, and computer-based technology and services.

A matrix organization was adopted in 1973 which recognized five disciplinary outcomes or research activities on one dimension of the matrix and five school outcomes or development-demonstration activities on the other dimension. The five school outcome components summarized the main ways in which LRDC expected to affect children and schools. Four of the components were curriculum areas: (1) Communication and Language, (2) Mathematical Thinking, (3) Scientific Inquiry and Problem Solving, and (4) Basic Learning Skills. The fifth component, Learning Environments and Classroom Behavior, was aimed at integrating the four curriculum areas into functional educational settings. In carrying out its work in these areas, the Center expected to make contributions to substantive and methodological knowledge in the following disciplines: (1) learning, developmental, and cognitive psychology; (2) sociology and social psychology; (3) measurement and evaluation; (4) computer science; and (5) instructional design and development.

As indicated by the matrix organization, the Center viewed research, development, implementation, and evaluation as a complex set of mutually dependent and interactive activities. The multiple professional roles were now systematized so that the individual professional could maintain his or her several identities within the overall framework of the Center. In 1975, LRDC and the University's Falk Laboratory School collaborated on establishing a new classroom where 50 children could receive individualized instruction under the new Self-Schedule System. At last the Center had evolved into a program that contained both research facilities and a laboratory school housed in its own building.

What has been accomplished in the first 12 years of the Center? The publication series alone contains 240 articles, many of which are major contributions to the field of education and related behavioral sciences. Field tests planned for the Fall of 1976 constituted a new phase of cooperation with schools in trying out basic instructional systems for reading, science, and mathematics. The IPI materials had already been disseminated throughout the country by Research for Better Schools, the federally funded educational laboratory located in Philadelphia which has been responsible for field testing and dissemination of several programs developed at LRDC. The Self-Schedule System and the comprehensive early learning program had been successfully implemented. The dimensions of individualization and adaptive education now included the pace or time, the method of presentation, and the social setting in which instruction took place. The accomplishments of LRDC are recognized and have been well documented. Clearly, it is one of the most successful of the research and development centers established primarily with federal funding during the expansive 1960s. Unlike many that were spawned during this period, LRDC continues to thrive as a vigorous research and development institution.

Wayne H. Holtzman

THE MODERN ERA OF FEDERAL
INVOLVEMENT IN EDUCATIONAL
RESEARCH AND DEVELOPMENT

As pointed out earlier, only since the Cooperative Research Act of 1954 has the Federal Government taken an active interest in educational research. For the first time in 1954, the Commissioner of Education was authorized by Congress to contract with universities and state agencies for research surveys and demonstration projects. Initial funding of one million dollars in 1956 was devoted primarily to mental retardation. Only after the shock of Sputnik and the passage of the National Defense Education Act in 1958 did the federal support of research accelerate. The major new curriculum studies in science and mathematics at the U. S. Office of Education were the direct result of this major legislation.

President Kennedy's New Frontier formed the basis for the great domestic programs under President Johnson several years later. John Gardner's task force on education in 1964 recommended a coordinated national research and development effort with the establishment of centers and regional laboratories throughout the country. LRDC was one of the four established in anticipation of the 1965 Elementary and Secondary Education Act. With Lyndon Johnson as President and John Gardner as Secretary of Health, Education, and Welfare, the Great Society Program was launched by an enthusiastic Congress. Twenty-five major bills and a score of minor ones dealing with education were enacted in 1965. The most significant of these was the Elementary and Secondary Education Act and the accompanying appropriation of over one billion dollars. While only 70 million dollars was appropriated for Title IV dealing with research and training (and 20 million dollars of this was for construction only), the stage had clearly been set for rapid expansion of federal involvement in education. Total appropriations for the U. S. Office of Education more than doubled each year from 1964 to 1966, reaching a figure of over 3 billion dollars. The only ominous note occurred in 1966 when a cut of 10.5 million dollars occurred in research. The Vietnamese War and social turbulence of the late 1960s were now entering in full force.

11

What happened elsewhere in the federal budget for research and development during these post-World War II years? In the 20 years from 1945 to 1965, federal appropriations for research and development in defense, atomic energy, space, and health grew from only 1.5 billion dollars to over 16 billion dollars. Most of this growth was in hardware areas, over 14 billion dollars in defense and aerospace industries. Most of the research efforts were undertaken by private industry. Among the universities, the top 25 succeeded in getting 60 percent of the federal money for research. Over 60 percent of the funds were spent in only five states—California, Massachusetts, New York, Illinois, and Maryland-District of Columbia. As these geographic and institutional imbalances became apparent, Congress and the general public grew more restless.

Federal support of research reached a peak in 1968, just prior to the change of administration from Johnson to Nixon. The variety and depth of activities were indeed impressive. Twenty-one research and development centers, 20 regional laboratories with special missions to develop products and interface with the schools, over 100 graduate training programs in educational research, and thousands of demonstration projects under Title III of the Elementary and Secondary Education Act represented a total federal investment approaching 200 million dollars a year. Sharp budget cuts in 1969, followed by disorganization and confusion within the federal education establishment, led to the dismantling of many of these programs during the early 1970s. In spite of some supporters in Congress, such as John Brademas, educational research and development suffered serious blows. The establishment of the National Institute of Education in 1971 only made it easier for those in search of a way to cut the budget. By 1975, even the curriculum development projects under the National Science Foundation were viciously attacked in Congress and reduced in scope.

Many of us are still reeling from these heavy blows received by educational research and development since 1968. Searching for scapegoats, we are often too prone to blame the Nixon administration or individual congressmen for the difficulties in which we find ourselves. Congress and other elected politicians largely reflect the

12

mood of the people. How has this mood changed in the past several decades? Significant clues as to what has happened can be found in a closer examination of social change in America over the past 20 years.

SOCIAL CHANGE IN AMERICA

What was America like 20 years ago when the first federal involvement in educational research and development was launched? Most of us can recall the quiet period following the Korean War when babies of the Great Depression were coming of age. Our optimistic pursuit of the Great American Dream was tempered only by fear of communism and the cold war. The stage had been set for social justice by the historic Brown decision on school desegregation. Only in the late 1950s were we rudely awakened by Russia's launching of Sputnik. The pace quickened in the early 1960s with the New Frontier and the Great Society. Most of us really believed that we could solve our social problems by pouring enough money and talent into the effort.

Rising expectations soon outpaced accomplishments. Shocked by the assassination of our young President, John F. Kennedy, followed by the killing of his brother and of Martin Luther King, we soon found ourselves in the midst of violence and uncertainty. Nowhere was this more evident than among college-age youth who formed the nucleus of the campus rebellion.

Social indicators of crisis started to rise steeply in 1964. While little or no change occurred between 1950 and 1960, by 1965 violent crime, the sale of handguns, births out of wedlock, the use of drugs, and mental illness were increasing at a rapid rate and, in some cases, have been doubling every four years since.

The pressures were especially acute on our university campuses, many of which doubled in size during the 1960s. Higher education was clearly a growth industry with bright future prospects, or so it seemed to many of us involved in its rapid expansion. It hardly seemed possible that there would ever be enough teachers for our schools, enough technology for our

13

curriculum needs, or enough education for an insatiable society striving to improve itself.

Changing values of the young during the late 1960s were of concern to many as evidence that American society was entering a new era. One of the most thorough studies of this phenomenon is the series undertaken by Daniel Yankelovich and associates, beginning in 1967. Supported initially by *Fortune*, CBS News, and the John D. Rockefeller III Fund, Yankelovich conducted a series of repeated interviews on college campuses throughout the country in order to document changing trends among college-age youth. In his later surveys, he added samples of youth aged 16 to 25 from several thousand households across the country in order to study the noncollege youth as well. Of the 19 large-scale changes in youth values and beliefs between the late 1960s and the early 1970s, as documented by Yankelovich, several are particularly significant in understanding public attitudes toward the federal support of research and development in education (Yankelovich, 1972, 1974).

In 1967, a central theme on campus was the search for self-fulfillment in place of a conventional career. There was growing criticism of America as a "sick society," and the value of education was severely questioned. New life styles and radical politics appeared together as part of the flowering campus rebellion. The universities and the military were major targets of criticism. A new naturalism had emerged in the counter-culture movement, placing emphasis upon sensory experience rather than conceptual knowledge, upon being rather than doing, and upon the community rather than the individual. Hypocrisy was rejected and only earned authority respected. The new naturalism deemphasized organization and technology.

By 1973, the central theme on campus had shifted back to finding self-fulfillment within a conventional career. Value of education was once again strongly endorsed, together with a strengthening of the work ethic on campus. While criticisms of universities decreased sharply with the disappearance of the campus rebellion, criticism of other major institutions, such as political parties and big business, continued and were taken up by working-class youth as well. Many of the new values dealing with moral norms, social values, and self-fulfillment spread from the college minority to the working-class young and general public. The noncollege youth of 1973 looked very much like the college youth of 1969. The severe economic recession of the past several years has sharpened these trends. Minority youth in particular have been disillusioned by higher expectations coupled with lower opportunities.

Yet another important social indicator of change in American society is the steady drop in the percentage of individuals in nationwide surveys who report that they are "very happy." As Campbell, Converse, and Rodgers (1976) at the Michigan Survey Research Center point out in their longitudinal surveys on the quality of American life, most of the decline in general sense of well-being takes place among the young and middle-aged and among the youth from affluent families since 1963. Just as the Great Society Program and the rapid expansion of research and development in education moved into high gear, the more articulate and influential segments of our society grew increasingly disillusioned and alienated. While the Vietnamese War and the change of administration in Washington may have played an important role in these events, the major social trends are too broad and deep to be accounted for in such simplistic terms.

By the early 1970s, most Americans were better off materialistically speaking than the previous generation, but they were hardly aware of it since rising expectations had overtaken accomplishments. Rising demands coupled with a crisis of belief in authority and a shrinkage of leadership have led to political apathy and inertia. Daniel Bell sees this loss of civitas and shared consensus as a deep moral crisis confronting America. Until this crisis is resolved by national leadership and renewed confidence in our social institutions, it is unlikely that there will be any significant improvement in public understanding and acceptance of educational research and development.

THE FUTURE CHALLENGE

Renewed federal support of research and development in education must await a new public mandate and administration. There are a number of unresolved problems peculiar to educational research that require close attention as we reorganize for the future. One of our greatest problems is how to define the product of our research and development in terms that the general public can understand and accept. A new piece of military hardware, a new technology for producing cheap energy, or even new forms of medical treatment are much easier to understand. Education is more like mental health—hard to define, hard to sell, and easy to mislead. Unfortunately, there is no clear consensus as to the goals of education and the priorities that should be attached to such goals.

A second problem concerns the immature state of the art in educational research. In spite of vigorous advances of the past several decades, currently available theory and knowledge are severely limited. We tend to focus upon techniques, method, and hardware because they are more definable and the research procedures can be more clearly specified. However, basic research and further theoretical advances like those underway in the Learning Research and Development Center are essential before significant new levels of educational practice can be implemented.

Public expectations were raised to unrealistic levels in the enthusiasm of the 1960s, leading in turn to disillusionment and rejection of educational research and development. Enthusiastic advocates of educational research were swept along with the Great Society programs, often assuring the public of great benefits to be received in return for modest investments over a short period of time. Just as many of our other major institutions in American society have been severely criticized and rejected by the alienated Americans of the late 1960s and early 1970s, so has educational research and development suffered. Strong demands for public accountability are important to consider in any future programs.

The explosive growth of educational research and development in the four-year period from 1965 to 1969 was understandably accompanied by mistakes and confusion. Big research and development organizations drew the criticism and envy of the many stakeholders in education who were felt left out by these developments. Vested interests quickly arose in defense of the new social organizations. Heavy dependence upon federal funds and the resulting political crosscurrents and instabilities distracted and demoralized the educational researcher and developer in all too many of these new institutes and programs.

Major programmatic research moves forward in a cycle requiring a minimum period of three to five years for completion. If longitudinal studies are planned to determine the enduring impact of an experimental educational program, the cycle may run considerably longer. Even specific, short-run projects usually require several years before significant results are obtained. Funding commitments for a period of years must be made at the start of a research and development program if it is to have sufficient stability for success to be possible. And yet, time and again the sponsoring federal agency places the entire enterprise in jeopardy by repeatedly forcing the project staff to spend an excessive amount of time justifying requests for annual continuation or for absorption of sharp budget cuts.

Educational research and development has never had an effective, broad-based constituency in Washington since few of its products have been readily accepted as making a real difference to the stakeholders in education—to school administrators, teachers, parents, and students. David Clark (1976) has called for a new coalition of diverse national organizations concerned with education to be built upon a reconceptualization of the role of research and development, decentralizing it and tying it more closely to educational practice. Coalitions are only effective when formed around an overriding shared interest in achieving a specific goal. The general retrenchment in education due to the presumed surplus of teachers, the beleaguered urban school systems, the leveling off of pupil enrollment, and the economic "stagflation" of the past three years has created a different set of interests than existed ten years ago. One must do more than extol the virtues of research and development to establish a broad coalition. Only when the direct benefits of such research are realized by the stakeholders will supporting coalitions emerge.

Given recent social trends, the state of the national economy, and past confusion and ambivalence concerning educational research and development, we shall be fortunate indeed if modest gains in the amount and stability of federal funding can be assured for the next several years. Meanwhile the outcomes of major programs such as those undertaken by the Learning Research and Development Center are beginning to have a strong impact in a significant number of schools throughout the nation. Many thousands of teachers and millions of students are now reaping the benefits of research and development of the past ten years. The accomplishments of the past decade are indeed significant in spite of deficiencies noted. As these achievements are strengthened and properly recognized, the renewed self-interest of the stakeholders in education can be stirred into positive action in support of more vigorous federal funding. But it will take time. It will take close attention to the major social changes in America. And it will take a concerted effort on the part of all of us.

REFERENCES

Campbell, A., Converse, P. E., & Rodgers, W. L. *The quality of American life.* New York: Russell Sage Foundation, 1976.

Chase, F. S. The mixed report card of the sixties. In *Educational research: Prospects and priorities.* Committee on Education and Labor, House of Representatives (Appendix 1 to Hearings on H.R. 3606 and related bills). Washington, D. C.: U. S. Government Printing Office, January, 1972.

Clark, D. L. Federal policy in educational research and development. *Educational Researcher*, 1976, *5*, 4-9.

Salmon-Cox, L., & Holzner, B. *The Learning Research and Development Center at the University of Pittsburgh: An assessment of organizational experience with educational R&D.* Unpublished manuscript, University of Pittsburgh, Learning Research and Development Center, January 1976.

Yankelovich, D. *The changing values on campus.* New York: Washington Square Press, 1972.

Yankelovich, D. *Changing youth values in the 70's.* New York: J. D. Rockefeller III Fund, 1974.

EDUCATIONAL RESEARCH AND CHANGE:
A STATE PERSPECTIVE

JOSEPH M. CRONIN
State Superintendent of Education
Illinois Office of Education

Diversity and complexity characterize education today, probably more than ever before. In this time of vast, intense, and accelerated change, problems, contradictions, and concerns abound. All states are faced with pressures for accountability at all levels of education. There are concerns for meeting the special needs of individual students—female and male, bilingual, minority, and the exceptional. There are concerns for the development and application of new techniques and materials for meeting current and changing student needs. Desegregation, declining enrollments, and lack of adequate revenue for financing schools can easily be added to the list of problems facing the states today.

As educational researchers, we assume that research can provide a foundation for problem solving in a changing society. Washington Irving once said, "There is certain relief in change . . . as I have found in traveling in a stagecoach, that it is often a comfort to shift one's position and be bruised in a new place." As State Superintendent in a highly complex and diverse state like Illinois, I have acquired a bruise or two. Change is not always comfortable, though it may be beneficial. Changes in our world not only affect education but also influence our research needs. My remarks at this symposium address some interrelated issues and suggestions about educational research and change from a state's perspective.

RESEARCH AND EDUCATIONAL POLICY

The first issue concerns the development of educational policy. Most of our current educational policy has not been developed by educators, which is also to say that it often has not

19

been influenced by educational researchers. Educational policy has been determined as a result of economic and political forces. Policy has been decided more often in the courtrooms than in research institutions. Obvious examples of such policy making are the court decisions related to the ways in which states finance their schools. Also, the desegregation/integration issue continues to be dealt with in the courts with a profound impact on schools and communities.

Educators and educational researchers must understand the policy implications related to cultural change. This implies the need for policy research that is designed to guide social action rather than contribute to knowledge in a specific discipline. There are problems, of course. One is that much research affecting policy is conducted by either economists, sociologists, or psychologists; their respective disciplines view the context of the investigation from a perspective different than that of education. Thus, a coalition of policy researchers may be needed. In this way, we can maximize the objectivity and usefulness of policy research in education.

To be useful to a state education agency, policy research must be continuous, current, and as immediately accessible as possible. Decisions made by state education agencies and state boards of education are most often in response to political pressures and in tight time frames. Research utilizing basic scientific inquiry modes often takes too long to answer difficult questions. For this reason, findings are usually synthesized from a series of related studies. We need basic research, but we also need educators involved in policy-related research.

There is another problem with research as it relates to decision making—a problem, however, that also has merit: The more research we have, the more evident it is that we have fewer definitive answers, while questions tend to become more numerous and exact in the process. Issues get clarified and sharpened, they fade away or emerge. New insights are developed as old assumptions are challenged. In all, it makes us more rational about the implications of the issues and the alternatives.

A specific example of this issue concerns the goals of the schools. Confusions here lie in the processes involved in establishing priorities and implementing programs, not in the goals themselves. We all want our children to be competent in reading, writing, and computation; to feel good about themselves as human beings; to be able to make value judgments; to be physically healthy and active; and to have an interest in learning which will be lifelong and rewarding to them and to society. We want them to understand and respect differences in people yet maintain their own individuality. We want them to develop skills which will earn them a living. All these things are considered goals for the schools. All are important.

Yet, the public schools cannot afford to be all things to all people. We need to identify priorities in goals. We need to identify the goals we can support with the human and fiscal resources we now have. We need to identify the learners of all ages who can benefit from the available resources. It may very well be that the most difficult task that school people have is to decide what they will *not* do.

In response to these needs—primarily a financially oriented response—schools all over the nation are developing competency-based tests in the basic skills. Researchers can measure and monitor what the reduction of education to such competencies will produce. The state education agency needs research to help it determine how a community can identify its needs and make responses appropriate to its own situation. Among other things, we must be aware of what real alternatives exist. These are value questions, of course, and the process of gaining consensus on goals is political. These are also researchable questions in many instances, and are ones that educational researchers must grapple with to help the state fulfill its responsibility for schooling.

IMPACT OF RESEARCH ON SCHOOLS

If research related to educational policy making is the first major issue from the state's point of view, the second issue is the impact of educational research on teachers and students. There are, for example, excellent studies on classroom organization, reading methods, computer-assisted instruction, development of curriculum products, teacher effectiveness, and so forth. From appearances, however, teachers and students have not been changed as a result of these studies. One of the reasons is that the benefits of the needed research on basic learning processes goes from the researcher back to the researchers. (For example, ERIC is not used by practitioners.) In any case, it is too much to expect teachers and administrators to translate the results of research into better practice as a result of reading journal articles. The problems identified by researchers are not always viewed as the problems of teachers. Similarly, the problems of teachers are not necessarily the problems of students.

Educational research is all too often not designed with teachers in mind. This is a serious problem because the value of educational research lies in its applicability for improving the learning of children. In all research, we have to ask how children and classrooms are involved. For example, research designed to lighten the workload of teachers and administrators is helpful, but it clearly must deal with the ensuing effects on students.

Educational research that focuses on the classroom as a laboratory needs further emphasis. Better collaborative models between the researcher and the practitioner are needed. University training programs that include research from a practitioner's point of view, that is, applied research that guides action or improves practice, must be given emphasis equal to that of research methodology. Results of such classroom studies must be shared with the public. The professional obligation of the researcher does not end with the publication of results in journals never read by the public. This is not to suggest that researchers must become political advocates for the results of their studies. It does suggest that change in research training must be considered if results are to be made more useful.

Although state education agencies do not teach children, the state's research needs are similar to that of the classroom. Research that leads to action is more relevant from the state's perspective. Currently, the major issues we see are desegregation/integration/busing; finance; declining enrollments; stopouts/dropouts/pushouts; responsibility education to counter discipline, crime, and truancy problems; and staff development. Research in these areas is clearly needed for the formulation of statewide policy making, legislation, and, in particular, program services and development.

With collaboration from other state researchers, including state teacher organizations, the Illinois Office of Education has conducted studies in school finance, declining enrollments, truancy, and absenteeism. Other studies include a statewide study of Illinois preservice teacher education in order to provide a data base for assessing and evaluating the more than 200 individual teacher education curricula offered in 61 institutions in Illinois.

School finance in Illinois underwent a significant reform in 1973. As a result, in 1976, we established a statewide commission of school finance researchers to evaluate the effects of the reform. The commission includes not only university and agency researchers but legislators and state budget personnel.

Every year the research staff of our state office collaborates with the state association for teachers and the state association for school boards on a study of teacher salaries and salary policies. Thus, current data is accessible to all groups during negotiations of new salaries and policies.

These are a few practical examples of how the state collaborates with diverse groups on research studies having a decision or policy focus. I should also point out that the Illinois Office of Education is served by a Research and Evaluation Advisory Council which is composed of state and university researchers. Advice and counsel to the agency's staff in research, evaluation, policy analysis, and planning are vital to our maintaining an objective perspective.

PRODUCTION AND UTILIZATION OF KNOWLEDGE

The next issue addresses the production and utilization of knowledge. Along with the production of new knowledge, there must be more effective dissemination and utilization of existing knowledge. Research results must be translated into practice and communicated to the practitioners.

The development of dissemination models is crucial to knowledge production and utilization efforts. The development of "broker" models is also needed. By broker models, I mean alternative ways in which staff in state education agencies can assist in getting research services to the schools. One way is to develop a cadre of university educational researchers who, as a public service to schools, will work part-time in the schools on a research problem identified by district or school personnel. These research services can be the conduct of research as well as the dissemination and translation of available knowledge into practice. It can be the state's role to broker the right set of researchers to the school or district needing assistance. This, of course, requires close collaboration of agency personnel with university researchers. All parties will benefit from such collaboration.

In general, however, the educational needs from the state perspective can be most effectively met when educational researchers and state education agency personnel collaborate. Although a state education agency is not mandated to play leadership roles, increasingly many are trying to do so largely because the image of regulator, evaluator, or bookkeeper is less productive than the more aggressive leadership image.

Collaboration of state education agency personnel with state educational researchers can take place in the following areas: (1) building and maintaining a useful data base for the schools and the state in general; (2) disseminating research findings to the schools; (3) assisting school personnel in the utilization of existing research findings and data retrieval; (4) serving as a liaison between researchers and practitioners; (5) providing support for the conduct of studies by university personnel, often at the request of the state education agency; and (6) assisting school personnel in terms of needs assessment, planning, and evaluation.

Collaboration of university educational researchers with those researchers within the state education agency is essential. The sharing of resources and expertise enhances the research effort including utilization of results. Collaboration of state researchers with those from the state professional organizations and other organizations and state agencies enhances the possibility that diverse perspectives will be considered and that data needs for differing purposes will be served more efficiently.

A state agency must not only provide developmental assistance to schools, but it must also be involved in the development of plans and policy recommendations for the consideration of the State Board of Education. It is obvious that both missions require the collection, interpretation, and presentation of research findings as a basis for decision making.

DATA SYSTEMS FOR DECISION MAKING

The last issue I wish to discuss today relates to the development of a usable data base for decision making at the state level. I am talking about developing management information systems relative to pupils, programs, personnel, finance, and facilities. Data systems are needed which are comprehensive yet require the least reporting burden for the local districts. Data systems are needed which provide ready access and are standard enough to be available for complex research manipulations as well as simple statistical description. These data bases require a merging of expertise from educational researchers, computer programmers, systems analysts, and management information specialists. These data bases are needed to determine the status of education, which, once described, will force us to ask if where we are is where we should be. These pursuits establish a climate for change; educational researchers can help us to ask the right questions, and their findings can help us to decide where it is that we should be going.

Perhaps the issues I have discussed are obvious to you, but frequently it is the "obvious" which is easily, quickly, or even defensively ignored. The issues and observations are very real, very significant, and very important if, in fact, we hope to focus upon the impact of educational research upon state education needs.

In sum, there has to be a dialogue between researchers of one discipline and another. There has to be a dialogue between the researchers and the educational practitioner. There has to be a dialogue between the researcher, practitioner, and the decision makers. There is a need for a partnership. A true measure of our success is whether people's lives *are* improved—in and during the course of their formal schooling—and continue to improve as they apply what they have learned to their postschool lives.

THEORETICAL RESEARCH AND SCHOOL CHANGE[1]

JACOB W. GETZELS
R. Wendell Harrison Distinguished Service Professor
University of Chicago

Educators and educational researchers themselves are extraordinarily skeptical about how research—particularly theoretical research—bears on the operation of schools. Here, as one instance for many, is a not atypical statement emanating from a prominent educational research center: "The fact is basic research produces only tiny 'bits' of knowledge about an infinitely complex world. Given time, such incremental gains in knowledge may have some effect on practical situations, but schoolmen have long been aware that research findings usually have little practical bearing on the actual operation of schools" (*R&D Perspectives*, 1969, p. 1).

It is on grounds such as this—that knowledge from research has little effect on changing school practices—that support for theoretical work has been sacrificed for other more applied activities, which presumably have instant bearing on changing our schools. Not only is the expenditure for research and development in education less than in any other field—for example, in health it is 4.7 percent of the budget, in agriculture 1.5 percent, while in education it is only .4 percent—but worse, when funds are cur-

---

[1]Parts of this chapter are based on "Paradigm and Practice: On the Contributions of Research to Education," a paper presented at the American Educational Research Association annual meeting, Los Angeles, California, February 1969; "Problem Finding," the 343rd Convocation Address, The University of Chicago, *The University of Chicago Record*, 1973, 7(9), 281-283; "Images of the Classroom and Visions of the Learner," *School Review*, 1974, *82*, 527-540; "Educational Administration Twenty Years Later: 1954-1974," keynote address at the Conference of the University Council for Educational Administration, Columbus, Ohio, April, 1975; and "Paradigm and Practice: On the Impact of Theoretical Research in Education," paper prepared for the National Academy of Education, 1976.

tailed, as they were for the National Institute of Education in 1974, the first and surest victim is the already scant support for research and theoretical work (Stiles, 1972; Stivers, 1973).

I shall argue that the substance of the assertions that research, and especially theoretical research, has little impact on the schools is in egregious error; contrary to such assertions, theoretical research has had manifest impact on school change.

My argument proceeds in three parts. First, I shall show that knowledge produced by theoretical research has had profound effects on altering the curriculum and modes of instruction. Second, I shall show that far from contributing only tiny bits of inapplicable knowledge, as is charged, theory-oriented research contributes to broad conceptions or paradigms of the human being and thus provides the critical contexts for educational policy. Third, I shall show that the conceptions and paradigms enter into the preparation of school personnel, and, in fact, as the conceptions are altered, their preparation is altered.

Before I turn to the argument proper, a word must be said about the term theoretical research. All categories and names for types of inquiry are bound to be imprecise. But whatever the terminology and despite the borderline cases, the distinction between basic and applied, theoretical and practical, conclusion-oriented and decision-oriented holds, if only for analytic purposes (Cronbach & Suppes, 1969). In theoretical research, the aim is primarily comprehension and conceptualization; in applied research, it is primarily manipulation and control. No value judgment is intended regarding the necessity of one type of inquiry over another. Each has a characteristic function, and each obtains stimulation from the other. There is an exchange between the two; the relation is not linear but multidirectional, not sequential but organic.

THEORETICAL RESEARCH AND CURRICULUM AND INSTRUCTION

I now turn to the first part of my argument; that is, theoretical research studies have had powerful effects on school change.

Rather than arguing the issue in only general terms as has been done so often, I shall attempt to demonstrate this most simply by citing specific illustrative studies that have had manifest effects on changing the curriculum and the mode of instruction.

Consider, as a first instance, the effect upon the curriculum of Thorndike and Woodworth's (1901a, 1901b, 1901c) research on the doctrine of formal discipline or more narrowly on transer of training—research which was by no stretch of the imagination development, demonstration, or dissemination. It will be recalled that according to the doctrine of formal discipline, the mind was viewed as though it were a body, and the training of the mind was seen as analogous to the training of the body (Hugh, 1898). This doctrine, which rested securely on tradition, authority, and common sense, was used to justify Latin and Greek in the curriculum since they provided manifestly arduous mind-building exercises. As a representative text of the period explained: "The study of the Latin language itself does eminently discipline the faculties and secure to a greater degree than that of the other subjects we have discussed, the formation and growth of those mental qualities which are the best preparation for the business of life" (see Thorndike, 1913, pp. 360-361).

The doctrine of formal discipline had of course been called into question before, notably by the Herbartians. But Thorndike and Woodworth's experiments had enormous influence on education by demonstrating empirically that the mind just did not work that way. The findings were widely cited by the curriculum makers and contributed to profound alterations in the course of studies in the schools. One example among many is the article on curriculum that appeared in the May 1909 issue of the influential journal *Education* (Horne, 1909). The article is entitled (and the title makes precisely the point of my argument) "The Practical Influence of the New Views of Formal Discipline." It first summarizes the results of the experiments and then states (and compare this with the earlier remarks regarding the study of Latin as the best preparation for the business of life): "The Latin grind in the secondary school is left to justify itself as a matter of formal discipline. But now the ground is swept from under it. We have nothing to anticipate in consequence but a necessary decline in the percentage of students who study Latin" (p. 616). Further, anyone who doubts the contribution of theoretical work to school change should examine several texts on the place of Latin and Greek as school subjects a decade before and a decade after the appearance of Thorndike and Woodworth's studies (see Colvin, 1913, pp. 215-216).

Consider next, and more briefly, the impact on the mode of instruction of the apparently simple and irrelevant little study by Lewin, Lippitt, and White (1939) on how children behave in a club when faced with different kinds of club leadership. The observations showed that the behavior was a function of whether the leader was "autocratic," "democratic," or "laissez-faire," and it is doubtful that those who use the terms today to describe modes of instruction give their source a second thought. The words autocratic, democratic, and laissez-faire became part of the educational vocabulary as if they had been given by the good Lord at the Creation, instead of by a little piece of basic empirical research in Iowa during the 1930s.

Within several years after the study was reported, scores of treatises, textbooks, and school programs applied the findings to education. The physical conformation of classrooms was changed to provide for "democratic" rather than "autocratic" pupil-teacher relations, a subject to which we shall return in due course. Suffice it here only to ask: Was there any educator of the past generation (or for that matter of the present generation) who was not made aware of the effects of these styles of instruction on the "group dynamics" of the classroom?

None of this is to say that the vocabulary and point of view were necessarily as salutary as their proponents claimed. My point is a different one. Although I do not want to get into a silly dispute about whether theoretical or practical inquiry is more influential (my contention of course is that they are symbiotic and neither should be sacrificed for the other), I cannot help wondering whether dollar for dollar (if by no other criterion) there are many development or dissemination activities that have had a greater impact on school change than this basic study.

Finally, consider a more recent instance—the impact on both the curriculum and mode of instruction of Piaget's theoretical work on cognitive development. Indeed, consider the impact only of the research on conservation. Science teaching is a case in point. For instance, an entire issue of the *Journal of Science Teaching* in 1964 was devoted to the influence of Piaget's studies on the teaching of science. Another example is Karplus' (1964) two efforts to improve science instruction at the elementary school level. Both efforts had their source in Piaget's theoretical work.

Karplus' first effort was to produce curriculum material that was consonant with Piaget's stages of cognitive development and would help children reach the formal operational level. One of the topics, for example, was "Material Objects." Here the children became aware of what is material in the environment and the conservation properties of material objects.

The second effort was to help the teachers acquire a view of the stages of the child's intellectual development so that their science instruction would be calibrated to the stages. This was done by introducing the teachers to Piaget's work. Karplus writes: "I think the conservation of volume study is one of the most impressive demonstrations that any teacher can carry out with children of age five, six, or seven. Those teachers to whom we have suggested this study and who tried it have been amazed. They would not have believed the results ahead of time" (1964, pp. 236-237).

Who would have thought that the theory-instigated investigation of children's ability to tell whether the volume of water in one glass tube was the same as that in another glass tube would one day be a significant influence on our schools? And would a question by a government funder regarding the practical utility of Piaget's study when it was being done (and of scores like it that I could cite) have been to the point?

I am reminded in this respect of the interchange between Faraday and Gladstone (Chandrasekhar, 1975). Faraday was working on the problem of electromagnetic induction, on which the electric dynamo was later to be based. Quite typically, his investigations were looked upon as only "theoretical" and useless by many of his more pragmatic contemporaries, including Gladstone, who was then Chancellor of the Exchequer. On one occasion when Faraday was describing his work, Gladstone broke in to ask impatiently, "But after all, what *use* is it?" Faraday's response was, "Why, Sir, there is every possibility that you will soon be able to *tax* it" (p. 107).

THEORETICAL RESEARCH AND EDUCATIONAL POLICY

I come now to the second issue; that is, to the charge that even when it is productive, theoretical research—or as it is often scornfully referred to, "merely theoretical research"—provides only tiny bits of knowledge without relevance to the broad policy problems of education. Nothing, it seems to me, can be further from the case. It is precisely theory-oriented inquiry that alters the general conceptions, or what Kuhn (1962) calls the *paradigms* of the human being, which in turn provide the critical contexts within which one deals with the broadest problems of educational practice. Consider in this regard only policy decisions regarding the architecture of the classroom as symbolic of more profound but less immediately visible changes in the school.

Almost within sight of my office are four school buildings. In the first, dating from the turn of the century, the spaces called classrooms are rectangular in shape, the pupils' chairs are bolted to the floor, and the teacher's desk is front and center. In the second building, dating from the 1930s, the classrooms are square, the pupils' chairs are movable, and the teacher's desk is out of the way in a corner. In the third building, dating from the 1950s, the classrooms are also square but the pupils' desks are trapezoidal in shape so that when placed next to each other they form a circle, and the teacher's desk has vanished. In the fourth building, there is a classroom constructed in the 1970s that is four times the size of the ordinary classroom and has no teacher's or pupils' desks but, instead, is filled with all manner of odds and ends from finger paints to Cuisenaire rods. If one were not told it was a classroom, this space might be mistaken for an overgrown playroom or a warehouse full of children's paraphernalia.

Since architectural space or form presumably follows from the function for which it is intended, and since the function—teaching and learning—is presumably the same for all four classrooms, why are there these obvious differences among them? To be sure, if one looks into the classroom in operation, the differences often disappear. But this is not the problem I am addressing. The problem is how to account for the original straight-row classroom represented by the bolted school chair and for the alterations in the classroom represented by the changing school chair. Is there some reason for the sequence of the different forms, or was the sequence merely accidental? Indeed, there is the more fundamental question: Why does any classroom have a particular architectural form?

The form of the standard straight-row classroom is usually attributed to the 19th century tradition of building and architecture, the physical requirements for lighting and ventilation, and the pedagogy of the time which emphasized pupil discipline (Sommer, 1969). The changes in the subsequent forms of the classroom are attributed to alterations in these architectural, physical, and pedagogical considerations. I do not wish to minimize these considerations, nor of course the social forces that were also at work (Cremin, 1961). But there was another factor, albeit a less manifest one, that may ultimately be a more decisive determinant of the classrooms we build. This is our conception of the learner.

In the early years of this century, a dominant—by no means the only, but surely a dominant—conception of the child as learner was that he was cognitively an empty organism learning primarily by trial and error when a specific response was connected to a specific stimulus through the operation of pleasure or pain. Researchers in the laboratory were connecting desired stimulus-response bonds of animals in cages, and teachers were connecting desired stimulus-response bonds of children in the classroom.

This description of the early conceptions of the learner is of course an oversimplification and somewhat a caricature, as it must necessarily be in so brief a sketch. And I need hardly add that I do not intend to derogate the historic achievement of the associationist view of learning. But the essential point remains: The prevailing conception of the learner was as cognitively a more or less empty organism associating stimuli and responses through the operation of rewards and punishments under the control of the teacher. Both what was to be learned (the stimulus) and what was learned (the response) were believed to be determined by the teacher.

It was no accident, then, that the prevailing classroom arrangements were teacher-centered. Typically, the classroom was rectangular in form with the teacher up front and the pupils in chairs rigidly fastened to the floor in straight rows facing forward so that they could not turn away from the presumed primary source of their learning experience—the teacher. Given the particular conception of the learner, what could be a more eminently sensible and practical learning environment? Indeed, John Dewey (1900, pp. 47-48) complained that when he was trying to furnish his new laboratory school at this time according to his different conception of the learner, he was unable to find any other kind of classroom furniture.

How, then, did we evolve from this sensible and practical straight-row classroom (and all that this symbolizes in curriculum and mode of instruction) to the more recent, apparently equally if not more sensible and practical, classroom without a teacher's desk and the pupils' movable chairs all over the place (and all that *this* symbolizes in curriculum and mode of instruction)? The transformation did not occur because someone just happened to have the happy idea that a change in the way a classroom looks might be a good thing, or, more to the point here, because there was any specific study showing that children in the movable chairs learned better than children in the old fixed chairs. There were of course many reasons. But an important factor that those who derogate the effect of theoretical research on school change ignore was the modification in our conception of the human being as learner as a result of theoretical research.

It became clear that the individual did not seem to experience what he was to learn as discrete stimuli. Instead he saw apparently discrete stimuli as belonging together. In the laboratory, three dots placed in a certain relation to each other were not seen as three separate dots but as a single triangle; and in the classroom, two pieces of information given separately by the teacher were brought together by the learner himself into a single idea not given by the teacher in the separate pieces.

Learning was conceived as not only a connective process but a dynamic cognitive and affective process as well. Personality theory was postulating that the human being was not psychologically an empty organism. On the contrary, an individual was a bundle of tumultuous conscious, preconscious, and unconscious forces that determined his behavior. What the learner would and would not attend to—what he or she would and would not learn—were seen as determined by these forces. From this point of view, the learner, not the teacher, was the center of the learning process. Experimenters in the laboratory became concerned with the relationship between the learner's personality and his perception and learning; and teachers in the classroom became concerned with the relationship between the learner's needs and his adjustment and insight in the school situation.

It was no accident, then, that the character of at least the ideal classroom took on a new conformation. The teacher's desk was shifted from the front of the room out of the way to the side, and the pupils' rigid chairs in straight rows, which had seemed so sensible and practical from the older conception of the learner, were replaced by movable chairs that could be shifted at will according to the requirements of the teachers and also, even more important, to the needs of the pupils.

The conception of the learner in the first period reflected an associationist view of behavior and in the second a personalistic view. In the period that followed, it reflected the emerging social-psychological and field-theory views. The child as learner was envisioned as a social organism, and learning as occurring in a field of interpersonal actions and reactions, each person in the classroom serving as a stimulus for every other person. As Wallen and Travers (1963) point out, the group climate studies, to which we have already referred, became "better known to education students than any other single piece of research" (pp. 474-475). Experimenters in the laboratory were concerned with such matters as interpersonal cohesion and communication networks, and teachers in the classroom with sociometric structure and group processes.

35

Changes concomitant with the conception of the learner as a social organism were introduced into the curriculum and into the architectural conformation of the desirable classroom. To specify only the latter, if learning is a social or group process, then a circular seating arrangement where everyone in the group must face everyone else (as before they had been forced to face only the teacher) is the most sensible and practical learning environment (as before the rectangular straight-row arrangement had been). This in fact became an ideally favored learning environment, as the arrangements of classrooms built at the time will attest.

We come now to the present. How did we get from the straight-row or even the circular classroom to the so-called open classroom? Despite their differences, the older conceptions of the learner had one basic paradigm in common: They were founded in a combination of the homeostatic model of self-maintenance and the drive or tension reduction theory of behavior. As Hilgard (1948) describes this position, "Without drives the organism does not behave and hence does not learn" (p. 78). There has been a growing discontent with this paradigm of behavior, at least as it is applied to learning and other forms of intellectual activity. To be sure, learning, thinking, problem solving, and intellectual exploration may be means by which to reduce certain drives. But they are not only that. They may also be ends in themselves, the organism acting to increase as well as to decrease stimulation.

Studies by Hebb (1949), Hunt (1960), Piaget (1952), and White (1959), among others, converge in showing that the central fact of growth and development lies not in the reduction of drives but in the spontaneous interaction with the environment. A child, whose bodily needs have all been satisfied, does not remain at rest; it is just then that its play and exploratory behavior are most active. Moreover, a conspicuous portion of adult life is devoted to activity that can be classified only as "art," "science," "adventure," or at another level "working at riddles just for the pleasure of working at riddles"—behavior that cannot be said to contribute to bodily maintenance through sastisfying primary drives and attaining states of rest (Berlyne, 1966).

From this point of view, the human being as learner is not, as the former paradigm would have it, like a mechanical calculating or information processing device that lies idle until sparked by some drive, stimulus, conflict, problem, or teacher goad; rather, the human being as learner is a vital cognitive entity that must be given an effective oppportunity to act cognitively if it is to function and remain vital. Human beings need not be driven to explore, to think, or dream, or to seek out riddles and problems for solution; they are intrinsically constituted to do just this. The learner is not only a stimulus-reducing and problem-solving organism but also a stimulus-seeking and problem-finding organism (Getzels, 1964, 1974, 1975).

Just as the spatial arrangements of the older classrooms were compatible with the then current conceptions of the learner, so are the spatial arrangements of the so-called open classroom compatible with this altered, newer conception of the learner. Quite typically, in accounts of efforts to institute an open classroom, the underlying assumption for such a learning environment is given. Barth (1972), for example, writes, "Children are innately curious and will explore without adult intervention" (p. 18). He describes the consequent altered spatial arrangements as follows: "The teacher in the open classroom organizes his classroom . . . to extend the range of possibilities children can explore. . . . While in the traditional classroom the child learns at his desk, in the open school the locus of learning is where something of particular interest for the child happens to be" (p. 74).

I characterized the new classroom in the fourth building as appearing haphazard, looking like a playroom or warehouse, and not at all like a classroom. This is so if one regards the arrangements in the light of the traditional conceptions of the learner. If the same arrangements are regarded with the altered conception of the learner, what did not look like a classroom looks very much like a classroom and an appropriate place for learning. It is now the traditional arrangement of straight rows and rigid chairs that does not look like a classroom and seems an inappropriate place for learning, whether it is so or not.

I addressed the sequence of classrooms not to imply benefit of one classroom over the other. This is another matter; change is not necessarily progress. My intent rather was to illustrate in the concrete, if I may put it this way, the relation between theoretical research, conceptions of the learner, and school change.

THEORETICAL RESEARCH AND EDUCATIONAL ADMINISTRATION

I turn now to the third and final part of the argument; that is, that theoretical research and paradigms do not only have an impact on practice, but they enter into the preparation of the practitioners—whether the practitioners themselves realize it or not. As the paradigms change, their preparation changes. As a case instance for the general point, I shall refer to the preparation of educational administrators as reflected by the textbooks in the field.

During the first quarter of the century or so, the predominant view of administration was "scientific management" (Taylor, 1911). It held that good managers know exactly what they want done and see to it that it gets done in the best and cheapest way. The managers take away from their workers the responsibility for planning their work; managers must be in authority and provide appropriate incentives to stimulate their workers' efforts, for otherwise they will not do anything. Numerous textbooks, including those by Bobbitt, Cubberly, Strayer, and Reeder, applied these principles to educational administration. Cubberley (1916), for example, wrote in his book *Public School Administration* that the school administrator must plan the educational policy himself—and note this, for it will change drastically over the years—but "the details of this policy he may find it wise to keep to himself" (p. 145).

This view of educational administration was not the aberration of deluded or evil men or a perverse accident. However untoward it seems to us today, it was consistent with the prevailing conception of human behavior. As we have already seen, the dominant conception was that of an "empty" organism responding primarily to pleasure or pain, rewards and punishments—an organism that would do nothing unless impelled by the carrot of incentive or the stick of authority.

What came to be called the "human relations" view of administration developed during the second quarter century. This view held that good human relations was at the core of an organization, and that everyone in it from those in the most menial to the most exalted positions must "evoke each other's ideas . . . in pursuit of the common goal" (Metcalf & Urwick, 1940, p. 14). Support for this view came from the work in industry of Elton Mayo (1933) and Roethlisberger and Dickson (1939), among others, and more especially in educational administration from the ubiquitous studies of democratic and authoritarian leadership to which I have already referred. The results of these studies were applied not only to the management of pupils by teachers but perhaps even more to the management of teachers by administrators.

There was an outpouring of textbooks for the preparation of school administrators from this point of view. Here, for example, is a sample of titles: *Practical Applications of Democratic Leadership, Human Relations in Educational Organization, Democracy in School Administration, Improving Human Relations in School Administration.* Typically, the last named volume describes the group leadership studies and admonishes the prospective administrator that the primary responsibility of an administrator is to see to it that "all individuals affected by any decision should have a share in determining its character and form" (Yauch, 1949, p. 16). This is a far cry from Cubberley's admonition to prospective school administrators a generation before that they would be wise to keep their plans and policies to themselves.

Although the principles of scientific management and of human relations were antithetical in point of view, their programs for preparing administrators had much in common. Administration was conceived as a vocation or trade, not as a field of study; the orientation was prescriptive, not analytic. The texts espoused principles of what the administrator should do, not concepts he needed to understand.

At about mid-century, an altered view arose both of administration and of preparing administrators (see Getzels, Lipham, & Campbell, 1968). A compelling early argument for the altered

39

view was Herbert Simon's *Administrative Behavior*, published in 1945, which stated flatly that the prevailing prescriptions were "little more than ambiguous and mutually contradictory proverbs" and what was needed was a consistent and fruitful administrative theory (p. 240).

One of the earliest writers to deal with administration in theoretical terms was Chester Barnard. His remarkable treatise, *The Functions of the Executive*, which had been published in 1938, was rediscovered in the 1960s, or really discovered. So far as I could find, virtually no text in educational administration before the 1950s mentions this work; by the 1960s, hardly a text does not mention it.

There was a drastic shift in research during this period. In the first half-century, research in educational administration consisted mainly of status studies and collections of opinion. Later there was a marked transformation; considerable research had its source in theoretical propositions and applied the methods and concepts of the behavioral sciences. To grasp the difference, one need but compare the articles in the journals of the 1930s and 1940s with those in the *Journal of Educational Administration* and the *Educational Administration Quarterly*, both of which were founded in this period.

The most telling analysis, however, is to trace the introduction of the new ideas from the emerging theoretical research and treatises into the successive editions of the same text written by the same author or authors. In a sense, this analysis has the logic and rigor of a controlled experiment; we are keeping authorship constant and observing over time the impact of theoretical work in educational administration on the instruction of school administrators.

I shall use for my analysis the case of the formulation of the social process model of educational administration (Getzels, 1952; Getzels & Guba, 1957; Getzels et al., 1968; Getzels, 1969), not because it is the most notable instance of the argument I am making, but because I happen to be most intimately acquainted with this model. Consider a text that went through two editions. In the first edition (Morphet, Johns, & Reller, 1959), there were two references of a sentence each to the formulation of a model, one of which described it as "very limited" (p. 66). In the second edition, eight years later, it is presented in some detail, and described as "a model . . . which has been extremely fertile . . . [and] has already become a classic" (Morphet et al., 1967, pp. 67-68). The point here is not the merit of any particular model, least of all this one. The point is rather that there are manifest changes in the preparation of school administrators—changes having their source in basic research and theory.

Consider next a text that went through three editions. In the first edition (Knezevich, 1962), the last chapter, which included a description of the model, was entitled "Toward the Emergence of a Theoretical Framework for the Study of School Administration." It dealt briefly, almost hesitantly, with theory and its value for administration, as if the author was uncertain about its import. There is nothing hesitant or uncertain about the second and third editions. By the second edition (Knezevich, 1969), seven years after the first, the chapter originally entitled "Toward the Emergence of a Theoretical Framework . . ." had been retitled firmly "A Theoretical Framework for the Study of Educational Administration." Indeed, the text goes further and now adds a chapter entitled "Models in Educational Administration."

Consider now a last example—this from a text that has gone through four editions. The first edition (Campbell, Corbally, & Ramseyer, 1958) contains sections on the salary schedules of administrators, information about tenure and security, a list of associations and affiliations that the new administrator might face in a community (the text names three dozen such organizations), advice on how to choose which organization to join, and so on. There is no mention of theory, models, conceptual schemes, or the like.

In the second edition (Campbell et al., 1962) four years later, the sections on salary schedules, tenure and security, organizations and affiliations, and such remain. But a new chapter has been inserted on the social process model, with a section on its implications for administrative practice. By the fourth edition, nine years later, the foreword emphasizes that what the new administrator must learn and will find most useful are *concepts* of administration (Campbell, Bridges, Corbally, Nystrand, & Ramseyer, 1971,

p. xiv). The sections on salary schedules, tenure and security, associations and affiliations, and such have disappeared from the text entirely. A substantial section entitled "Theory in Administration" has been added—a section citing with approval Dewey's dictum that "theory is in the end . . . the most practical of all things" (Dewey, 1929, p. 17). The social process model is now presented in full, and a number of its concepts are applied to explicating certain problems that face the administrator.

The introduction of theoretical work into the texts for the preparation of administrators was of course not confined to this model. If one assumes, as I think one may, Barnard, Simon, and Parsons as the patron saints of organizational and administrative theory of the period, similar changes are observed. To cite only the text that went through four editions, the index to the first edition gives no references to Parsons or to Simon and only one to Barnard; in the fourth edition there are five page references to Parsons, six to Simon, seven to Barnard. In the first edition, Barnard's theoretical views are allotted exactly one sentence; by the fourth edition they receive an exposition of several pages. I need hardly repeat that I am pointing to the influence of theoretical research on *changes* in preparing school administrators; whether the changes were also improvements is an issue beyond the scope of the present observations.

A final word lest there be a misunderstanding. I am not of course contending that research other than theoretical, including research informed by immediate classroom and school problems, is not needed or is without effect. I am not doing anything of the kind; such research and development are manifestly of value. They require no defense. Even Gladstone understood their use, and so do the Gladstones of our time. But in light of the unqualified assertions that theoretical, or as it is invidiously called "merely theoretical," research has little impact on school change, and the increasing sacrifice of theoretical work for presumably more practical activities, in a symposium dedicated to research and development and school change, I thought it might be useful to explore the view that even with respect to school change there may ultimately be, to paraphrase Dewey, nothing more practical than research that is "merely theoretical."

REFERENCES

Barnard, C. *The functions of the executive.* Cambridge, Mass.: Harvard University Press, 1938.

Barth, R. S. *Open education and the American school.* New York: Agathon Press, 1972.

Berlyne, D. E. Curiosity and exploration. *Science,* 1966, *153,* 25-33.

Campbell, R. F., Bridges, E. M., Corbally, J. E., Nystrand, R. O., & Ramseyer, J. A. *Introduction to educational administration* (4th ed.). Boston, Mass.: Allyn & Bacon, 1971.

Campbell, R. F., Corbally, J. E., & Ramseyer, J. A. *Introduction to educational administration.* Boston, Mass.: Allyn & Bacon, 1958.

Campbell, R. F., Corbally, J. E., & Ramseyer, J. A. *Educational administration* (2nd ed.). Boston, Mass.: Allyn & Bacon, 1962.

Chandrasekhar, S. Shakespeare, Newton, and Beethoven, or patterns of creativity. *The University of Chicago Record,* 1975, *9,* 91-108.

Colvin S. S. *The learning process.* New York: Macmillan, 1913.

Cremin, L. *The transformation of the school.* New York: Knopf, 1961.

Cronbach, L. J., & Suppes, P. (Eds.). *Research for tomorrow's schools: Report of the Committee on Educational Research of the National Academy of Education.* New York: Macmillan, 1969.

Cubberley, E. P. *Public school administration.* Boston, Mass.: Houghton Mifflin, 1916.

Dewey, J. *The school and society.* Chicago: University of Chicago Press, 1900.

Dewey, J. *Sources of a science of education.* New York: Liveright, 1929.

Getzels, J. W. A psycho-sociological framework for the study of educational administration. *Harvard Educational Review,* 1952, *22,* 235-246.

Getzels, J. W. Creative thinking, problem-solving, and instruction, In E. R. Hilgard (Ed.)., *Theories of learning and instruction.* (Sixty-third Yearbook of the National Society for the Study of Education, Pt. 1). Chicago: University of Chicago Press, 1964.

Getzels, J. W. A social psychology of education. In G. Lindzey & E. Aronson (Eds.). *The handbook of social psychology* (Vol. 5). Reading, Mass.: Addison-Wesley, 1969.

Getzels, J. W. Images of the classroom and visions of the learner. *School Review,* 1974, *82,* 527-540.

Getzels, J. W. Problem finding and the originality of solutions. *Journal of Creative Behavior,* 1975, *9,* 12-18.

Getzels, J. W., & Guba, E. G. Social behavior and the administrative process. *School Review,* 1957, *65,* 423-441.

Getzels, J. W., Lipham, J. M., & Campbell, R. F. *Educational administration as a social process*. New York: Harper & Row, 1968.

Hebb, D. O. *The organization of behavior*. New York: Wiley, 1949.

Hilgard, E. R. *Theories of learning*. New York: Appleton-Century-Crofts, 1948.

Horne, H. H. The practical influence of the new views of formal discipline. *Education*, 1909, *29*, 614-623.

Hugh, D. D. Formal education from the standpoint of physiological psychology. *Pedagogical Seminary*, 1898, *5*, 599-605.

Hunt, J. McV. Experience and development of motivation: Some reinterpretations. *Child Development*, 1960, *31*, 489-504.

Karplus, R. The Science Curriculum Improvement Study: Report to the Piaget conference. *Journal of Research in Science Teaching*, 1964, *2*, 236-240.

Knezevich, S. J. *Administration of public administration*. New York: Harper & Row, 1962.

Knezevich, S. J. *Administration of public administration* (2nd ed.). New York: Harper & Row, 1969.

Kuhn, T. S. *The structure of scientific revolutions*. Chicago: University of Chicago Press, 1962.

Lewin, K., Lippitt, R., & White, R. K. Patterns of aggressive behavior in experimentally created "social climates." *Journal of Social Psychology*, 1939, *10*, 271-299.

Mayo, E. *The human problems of an industrial civilization*. New York: Macmillan Company, 1933.

Metcalf, H. C., & Urwick, L. *The collected papers of Mary Parker Follett*. New York: Harper & Row, 1940.

Morphet, E. L., Johns, R. L., & Reller, T. L. *Educational administration: Concepts, practices, and issues*. Englewood Cliffs, N. J.: Prentice-Hall, 1959.

Morphet, E. L., Johns, R. L., & Reller, T. L. *Educational administration: Concepts, practices, and issues* (2nd ed.). Englewood Cliffs, N. J.: Prentice-Hall, 1967.

Piaget, J. *The origins of intelligence in children*. New York: International Universities Press, 1952.

R & D Perspectives. Eugene, Ore.: Center for the Advanced Study of Educational Administration and the ERIC Clearinghouse on Educational Administration, 1969.

Roethlisberger, F. J., & Dickson, W. J. *Management and the worker*. Cambridge, Mass.: Harvard University Press, 1939.

Simon, H. A. *Administrative behavior*. New York: Macmillan, 1945.

Sommer, R. *Personal space: The behavioral basis of design*. Englewood Cliffs, N. J.: Prentice-Hall, 1969.

Stiles, L. J. Developing a research component for education. *Journal of Educational Research*, 1972, *65*, 197-203.

Stivers, P. NIE: Learning about Congress the hard way. *Educational Researcher*, 1973, *2*, 8-9.

Taylor, F. W. *Shop management*. New York: Harper & Row, 1911.

Thorndike, E. L. *Educational psychology* (Vol. 2). New York: Teachers College, Columbia University, 1913.

Thorndike, E. L., & Woodworth, R. S. The influence of improvement in one mental function upon the efficiency of other functions (I). *Psychological Review*, 1901, *8*, 247-261. (a)

Thorndike, E. L., & Woodworth, R. S. The influence of improvement in one mental function upon the efficiency of other functions (II). *Psychological Review*, 1901, *8*, 384-395. (b)

Thorndike, E. L., & Woodworth, R. S. The influence of improvement in one mental function upon the efficiency of other functions (III). *Psychological Review*, 1901, *8*, 553-564. (c)

Wallen, N. E., & Travers, R. M. W. Analysis and investigation of teaching methods. In N. L. Gage (Ed.), *Handbook of research on teaching*. Chicago: Rand McNally, 1963.

White, R. W. Motivation reconsidered: The concept of competence. *Psychological Review*, 1959, *66*, 297-333.

Yauch, W. A. *Improving human relations in school administration*. New York: Harper & Row, 1949.

RESEARCH ON CHILD DEVELOPMENT: IMPLICATIONS FOR SOCIAL CHANGE[1]

ALBERTA E. SIEGEL

Professor of Psychology

Stanford University School of Medicine

I have had the great personal privilege of being Ralph Tyler's friend since 1957, when my husband Sidney Siegel was a Fellow at the Center for Advanced Study in the Behavioral Sciences. Ralph was the Director. He had been with the new Center since its planning year in 1953 and had greeted the first class of Fellows at the new building on the Stanford campus in 1954. My part-time teaching at Stanford during my husband's year at the Center left me plenty of time to enjoy the Center and to make friends among the Fellows and staff and their families.

We were told that being selected as Fellow implied that you were ranked in the top five percent of your field for your age group. Having been trained in developmental psychology, which at that time was heavily dominated by theories of personality, I felt sure that these selection procedures meant that Fellows were being chosen for certain personality qualities like assertiveness, ambition, creativity, persistence, and competitiveness. I wondered what it would be like to bring 50 of these individualists together in the same small institution. It seemed clear to me that the institution which resulted from assembling them would be a tense, fast-moving, electric, hustle-bustle sort of no-nonsense place.

So it was a surprise for me to visit the Center that Ralph Tyler directed. It was calm, peaceful, slow-paced, friendly, pleasant, and serene. And the Fellows who arrived there quickly became noticeably calmer, slower paced, friendlier, pleasanter, less assertive, and less competitive as persons. The competitiveness I observed was

[1] In the preparation of this paper, I have consulted with Preston Cutler, Ronald Haskins, and Fred Volkmar. Each has offered helpful comments; none is responsible for my remarks, opinions, and errors.

principally in the sports arena. The Fellows' persistence was expressed in a lot of writing and in lengthy and intense conversations; books and articles and good talk flowed at the Center in a never-ceasing torrent, year after year.

Like every social scientist who observed the Center, I thought a lot about this remarkable institution that Ralph and his colleagues had created. It did just what it was meant to do, a claim that few social institutions can make. The Center facilitated communication across disciplinary boundaries. It advanced the work of leading scholars in the behavioral sciences. What seemed remarkable to me was that the Center achieved these goals while damping down the personal characteristics which its Fellows had developed in order to achieve entry to the ranks of leading scholars and while enhancing other personal characteristics which had not been so evident in other settings. At the time, I said "Ralph Tyler is making me a Lewinian," for in my field it was Kurt Lewin (1935) who had argued most persuasively for the influence of the immediate environment on the behavior of the persons in that environment. Ralph had created a setting in which personalities changed.

I had the opportunity to verify my hypothesis when I was invited to be a Fellow at the Center in 1961, and again when I was asked to stay on for an extra year in order to finish the work my husband had left incomplete at his death. My observations thus spanned three groups of Fellows. All three groups were amiable, mutually supportive, and sociable. Work moved along in a relaxed atmosphere in which there was always the opportunity for conversation and for exploring new ideas with new friends.

To anyone who believes in personality as a central fact of human existence, it is always a shock to meet a Center friend at his home institution, especially in his office at his university. His pace has quickened. His face has become tense. His movements are less athletic and graceful. His style of dress has become more conventional and less attractive. His conversation has a staccato quality. He glances nervously at the telephone, which usually has several buttons with lights flashing. Whatever personality is, people display it more favorably at the Center Ralph created than they do in their native habitat. And sometimes the man seems to realize that the contrast is unfavorable—perhaps my dismay appears on my face—for I catch him casting a longing glance at a small redwood cube with a silver top, a memento given to all Fellows, which is displayed casually but proudly on his desk. I remember that we are now in an "office," whereas when I knew this man at the Center he was working in a "study." And there was no telephone at all in that study, thanks to Ralph's thoughtfulness.

It has become commonplace in the mid-1970s to refer to the decade of the 1960s as "optimistic." The word is used pejoratively. The implication is that facts were not being faced squarely back then. As one of the optimists of that era, I want to say that we were optimistic because of facts and observations, not in spite of them. My experience at the Center was one major basis for my optimism. To me it was a demonstration that new institutions can be created to meet new needs. It taught me that old wine changes when it is poured into new bottles. I extrapolated from my thinking about the Center to my thinking about children. If people settled into middle age can change favorably when brought to a new institution, and can modify habits which have been heavily reinforced for long periods, then what about young children? Their reinforcement histories are briefer, their habits of responding are less set. We ought to be able to create or modify institutions serving children with effects even more remarkable than those observed at Ralph's Center.

My experiences at the Center prepared me for the decline we have witnessed in the belief in personality as a major explanation for social behavior. Today behavioral scientists are less likely to invoke notions like ambitiousness, creativity, status-striving, or even intelligence in order to account for the behavior of children and adults. We have been influenced by Walter Mischel's writings (1968) about personality constructs, and we have also been influenced by our observations about the readiness with which habits change when environmental cues and reinforcement schedules are altered. We have become more attentive to the situations in which people find themselves, and to the forces in those situations which elicit certain behaviors and which inhibit or neglect others. This is a viewpoint that makes us interested in social institutions and how they operate. It is a viewpoint that can be either "optimistic" or "pessimistic" depending on how readily social institutions can be changed.

ENVIRONMENTAL INFLUENCE ON DEVELOPMENT

In my professional lifetime, notions of personality and stability of habits entered into developmental psychology through ideas about critical periods. Some members of earlier generations thought that children turned out the way they did because of preformed structures of personality. The changes that were observed in childhood and adolescence represented the "unfolding" of a blossom which was already formed when the child was born. Changes represented maturation toward a predestined goal. Some children were born to be mean, some were born to be criminals, some were born to be stupid, and some were born to be geniuses.

This viewpoint was replaced by a view that children are influenced by their life experiences, and that the influence is especially important during stated critical periods. In this, we were greatly influenced by the writings of Erik Erikson (1950). He interpreted the discoveries of embryology to a generation of students of personality development. The embryo develops in utero along an orderly plan. New structures appear and grow according to a predictable timetable. Biological "insults" to the embryo can alter the plan. If the mother has certain illnesses early in the pregnancy, or if she ingests certain substances, the developing embryo is damaged. Although conceived with a perfectly good genetic endowment, the afflicted infant is born deaf, blind, or without limbs. It is not this child's heredity but the prenatal environment which has determined his or her fate. The notion of a critical period arose from observations that the same illness or the same ingested substance did not have the same effect on the fetus late in pregnancy as it had early in pregnancy. Only when the insult occurs at a specified interval of time in the pregnancy is the child damaged in the specified ways. If the intrauterine environment was healthy for the developing embryo and fetus during the critical period, from then on the fetus was apparently protected from damage to the structures that emerged during that period.

Erikson suggested that embryological development is a metaphor for personality development postnatally. At a given time in personality development, a given feature of personality is scheduled to emerge and become stabilized. This will happen in an ordinarily supportive environment. But if the environment is not hospitable to the emergence of that personality quality at that time, the quality will not appear on schedule and it may never appear subsequently in a truly healthy form.

I will not bowdlerize Professor Erikson's theory by suggesting that maternal indifference and blundering have the same effect on a baby's potential for developing a sense of trust in others that Thalidomide might have had on the embryo's potential for developing arms during the earliest weeks of life. Professor Erikson has been specific and eloquent in pointing to the precursors to the development of any particular quality of personality and to the necessity for further supports if that quality is to mature into adult forms in the years after the critical period (Erikson, 1968, 1975). The very term "critical period" does not come so much from Erikson's writing as from the writings of behavioral biologists, ethologists, and comparative psychologists. But anyone who has tried to deal fairly and kindly with a paranoid young adult who grew up in a disordered, isolated, and suspicious family can appreciate why an astute clinician would conclude that when an infant's life experience makes him fearful, suspicious, and distrustful, then that infant is launched on a life course in which those tendencies may well persist and be reinforced over subsequent years. Erikson's ideas, eloquently stated, fell on receptive ears. We came to think of personality development as a series of lasting achievements, with each new achievement building on a secure base of earlier achievements.

This viewpoint made us sensitive to different features of the environment for children at different stages of development. The infant needs life circumstances that support the development of a sense of trust. The toddler needs circumstances that support the development of a sense of autonomy. When planning for adolescents, we should be thinking of ways to support identity development. In institutions for young adults, our concern should be with enhancing opportunities for developing capacities for intimacy. As we thought about changing institutions in order to improve children's lives, we thought of stages in the life cycle and how social forces can enhance or deflect progress through those stages.

My topic is the implications for social change which emerge from research in child development. In the era when personality development was our dominant concern, the implications for social change were clear. Since each level of development involves its own focal issue or developmental task, in planning for a social institution for a particular age group, such as a day care center for toddlers or a junior high school for adolescents, the planner should give central attention to that specific developmental task. The forces of the institution should focus on the developmental issue which is distinctive to the age group being served by the institution.

Our thinking was bolstered by our acceptance of Piaget's stage theory of cognitive development (1952, 1970). Whereas Erikson talked about stages in emotional-social maturing, Piaget talked about stages in the maturing of thought processes. He persuaded us that the thinking process of an infant are qualitatively different from those of the young child, and in turn the thinking processes of a school-age child are different yet. His work implied that the ways one ought to teach children to solve problems were specific to their developmental levels. Sensory-motor experiences are especially helpful to the infant, and concrete manipulations of specified teaching materials are especially helpful to the preschooler. Verbal constructs—teaching by talking—make sense for children at later stages of cognitive maturity. Piaget's theory does not contain any notion of critical periods for environmental inputs. But one can straightforwardly extend his theory to suggestions that instructional inputs must be matched to the developing structures of thought in specified ways, as Hunt (1961, 1964) and others have done (Lavatelli, 1968).

In the 1950s and even more in the 1960s, a large mass of research was stimulated by theories about critical periods, imprinting, and sensitivity to early experience. This research, summarized ably by Thompson and Grusec (1970), raised additional issues with respect to environmental influences on development.

With respect to human beings, the evidence for critical periods is strongest with respect to prenatal morphological development. The presence or absence of particular drugs, viruses, vitamins, hormones, ionizing radiation, etc. will affect the developing zygote, embryo, and even fetus and determine where it falls on the continuum of reproductive casualty. Will the zygote survive to term, and if it survives, will the infant be born well-formed and healthy? Birth defects such as cleft palate, absence of limbs, cranial malformations, and the like can be traced to specific prenatal insults at definable sensitive periods.

The evidence for prenatal influences on behavioral development is less clear than the evidence for morphological development. And the behavioral evidence to date is more convincing for animals than for humans. "In fact, it is only the positive findings coming out of the animal studies that give credibility to the conclusions drawn concerning human beings. Generally the work has been epidemiological and retrospective in nature" (Thompson & Grusec, 1970, p. 585).

As for postnatal influences on somatic development, this has not been a lively area of research during the period of speculation about critical periods. The effects of malnutrition in infancy childhood, and adolescence are being studied, especially when the malnutrition is during a discrete period like a famine or a war. Available data, however, have not produced a consensus about whether or not there are critical periods for nutritional inputs during growth. One would speculate, of course, as with any developing function, that the critical period for insults or deprivation is the period of most rapid growth of the function. This is why malnutrition during infancy arouses special concern for the developing brain, and malnutrition during infancy and adolescence arouses concern about the child's ultimate height.

We have more research about postnatal influences on behavioral development. The most convincing evidence bears on the lasting influences of early experiences. Put another way, the earliest period of postnatal life may be a critical period, setting the infant on a developmental path.

Imprinting on conspecifics has been discussed anecdotally for hundreds of years and was given theoretical focus by Lorenz

(1935) almost half a century ago. It has been demonstrated experimentally not only in birds but also in goats and sheep, and possibly it occurs in primates as well. Leiderman, Grobstein, Leifer, Klaus, Kennell, and others have studied the human equivalent of imprinting in the newborn nurseries in hospitals (see Klaus, Leger, & Trause, 1975; Klaus & Kennell, 1976), and their work has led pediatricians and pediatric nurses and social workers to reform the practices of newborn nurseries in hospitals, not only for well babies but also for sick prematures, to assure early and intense social contact between the newborn infant and his or her parents.

As with prenatal critical periods, the evidence for postnatal critical periods in behavioral development is more convincing for animals than for humans and comes primarily from studies with rodents, birds, dogs, and primates. The human data are primarily from field studies of naturally occurring deprivations, and they lack experimental elegance and rigor. But most developmental psychologists are now convinced that the information currently available about human infancy indicates lasting effects of experiences in the first year of life on temperament, mood, emotionality, and sociability. The lasting effects of enrichment and deprivation in infancy on intellectual development are not so clear either in animals or men.

We have some reason to think that the first 3 years of postnatal life may be a sensitive period for language development. This is especially interesting because language is the most uniquely human set of skills. By the first birthday, most children are speaking a word or two, are understanding much of the speech directed to them, are accurately decoding gestural communications, and are employing gestures and facial expressions in culturally defined ways. Fred Volkmar and I are studying gestural communication in very young children (Volkmar & Siegel, 1976) and we are finding how competent 1-year-olds are in reading the facial expressions and body movements of the significant people around them. We might speculate that the first year of life is a sensitive period for the development of receptive speech. By age 3, children are highly competent members of their linguistic community, having mastered the basics of productive speech. We do see long-term deficits in language in children who are deprived of language inputs in the first 3 years of life, and also in children who have no social-emotional reason to be attentive and responsive to the language around them. I am thinking of the linguistic deficiencies of institutionalized orphans, and the way these deficiencies resist remediation. Perhaps it is not stretching the concept too far to say that these observations suggest that the initial 3 years of postnatal life constitute a "critical period" for language development, but in doing so we must acknowledge that 3 years is a pretty long period and also that deficits in inputs must be major for the effects to appear in the deprived children. And we must note that at least one very serious and well-informed student of the matter (Lenneberg, 1967) put the critical period for language learning at a later point in human development, starting at age 2, and thought it extended over a 10-year span, to age 12. My reading of the literature leads me to think that lasting effects of early experience on language may be expected to be especially evident in the phonological and the nonlexical aspects of communication behavior: word pronunciation, vocal intonations and rhythms, gestural communication, proxemics, and the like.

There is clinical evidence that gender identity is established in the earliest years of life and resists subsequent change. The term "gender identity" refers to a person's self-awareness of being either a female or a male. Presumably gender identity emerges from the child's consistently being treated by parents, siblings, and others as being of a given gender, from the child's experiences of imitating and identifying with persons of the same gender, and from the child's interacting in complementary ways with persons of the other gender.

Very occasionally, an infant is born who is genetically of one sex but who is genitally ambiguous or gives the appearance of belonging to the other sex. This may be the result of prenatal hormonal influences. If the physician and parents initially assign the child to the other sex, eventually the error of initial sex assignment may become apparent and the physicians and parents may consider a sex reassignment, with concomitant surgical and hormonal treatments. Fortunately, such cases are rare. And not all of them have been studied by professional people with an interest in psychological development. Even when they have, there has been reluctance to scrutinize the child and his or her life experience too extensively in order to avoid additional sensitization or stigmatization. So the evidence is clinical, including observations in an office, self-report, and parental report. Clinical opinion is that sex reassignment is more difficult psychologically in the second postnatal year than in the first, and even more difficult after the child is 2 years old. Both the parents and the child struggle to negotiate the change to a new gender, with all that implies for naming, use of personal pronouns, toileting, dressing, choice of toys, cuddling, reciprocity in body adaptations, and so forth. When sex reassignment is attempted after age 3 or 4, the child remains convinced that his or her gender identity is the gender in which he or she was reared during the initial years of postnatal life. "By the age of three to four years, it is typically as difficult for an hermaphroditic child as it would be for an ordinary child, or an adult for that matter, to negotiate an imposed change of sex . . . the change is incompatible with a concordant change of gender identity" (Money & Ehrhardt, 1972, p. 179).

These psychologists at Johns Hopkins describe their findings in terms of a hypothesis about a critical period for gender identity formation. Anyone familiar with the extensive and profound socio-emotional learning that occurs during the first three years of life (Caldwell, 1967; White, 1975) can hardly be surprised that a child is firmly and probably unalterably established in a gender identity by the third birthday. To the extent that any of us may have failed to appreciate the significance of the early years of postnatal life in setting lasting patterns, this may reflect the selectivity of our research efforts rather than any misapprehension of observed realities (Siegel, 1967).

In brief, at present the evidence for critical periods centers on the prenatal 9 months and the initial years of postnatal life. When we turn to thinking about possible critical periods later in development, evidence is not yet sufficiently convincing to have produced any sort of consensus. Developmental psychologists are left with more research to do (Siegel, 1969). The notion of sensitive periods is so pertinent to our concerns, and the evidence as it bears on morphological development is so persuasive, that we must continue research which identifies the competencies which arise at various stages, the inputs which support their emergence, and how effective remediation can be if the sensitive period is allowed to pass without the appropriate supports (Stendler, 1952; Bronson, 1962; Caldwell, 1962). My guess is that the sensitive period is not only the time when the slope of the acquisition curve is steepest, but also the time prior to that when the precursor skills are being consolidated and the pertinent observational learning is accelerating.

SOCIAL PLANNING AND SOCIAL CHANGE

Where does this leave us in our thinking about the relevance of research on child development for social planning and social change? Clearly, if the early years of life are so significant for later functioning, we must be especially attentive to the social supports for infants and toddlers. This means we must be alert to maintain family life and to strengthen it (Siegel, 1973). There are implications for hospitals and medical practice (Vaughan & Brazelton, 1976), for day care centers, and for other institutions serving very young children.

My student Gail Levinson (1977) is comparing a 2-year-old child's day in a day care center with the same child's day at home, and one of the contrasts that seems to be emerging is that these children talk much more at home and are spoken to much more frequently. They are often silent at the day care center, and very few remarks are directed to them. We must wonder whether day care centers provide an optimal environment for language development. This concern becomes pointed when we examine the evidence that language development depends especially on lively communicative exchanges between the child and those who have special emotional meaning for him. Many day care centers do not foster strong emotional bonds between the staff and the young children, so that the child's motivation to attend to the speech of his caretakers at the center is in no way comparable to his motivation for communicative attentiveness at home with members of his family.

There can be no question that single parents need assistance in the very difficult task of rearing preschool children while simultaneously holding a job to support the family. My student Ivonne Heras has recently completed a dissertation (1976) studying 2-year-olds who have been in day care for either 2, 4, or 6 months, or who are new to day care. She observed these children at about a dozen day care centers in the Boston-Cambridge area and on the San Francisco Peninsula. None of these was a university-related day care center. I was interested to learn that about half of the children in her sample were from one-parent families. Usually the single parent was the mother, and almost always this woman was holding down a full-time job. It is clear that day care serves the needs of parents, and that these needs are undeniable. The task of early childhood educators is to assure that day care centers are so well attuned to the development of young children that they serve the children's needs directly, as well as indirectly through providing an essential supporting service for the parent. The year from the second to the third birthday is a year of rapid language development, and the 2-year-old child's many needs include input to support that development.

The most profound implication of what we know about the early years is that every child needs to be in a stable and caring environment. If the child's own natural parents cannot provide this, then permanent adoption is his best hope, and the earlier in life the better. At present, we can document the efficaciousness of adoption as an intervention on behalf of children more extensively than we can document the efficaciousness of any other intervention (cf. Mech, 1973; Skeels, 1965, 1966). Of all the professional people who are working to improve the lives of children, those who are working to effect adoptions and to avoid institutionalization or foster home placement of children are the ones who can be most secure in the knowledge that their interventions are backed by research findings.

What about development after the earliest years of life? What is the evidence for critical or sensitive periods, and what are the implications for social policy and social change? I have not seen clear evidence for critical periods that have their onset well along in the years after birth and then terminate at some subsequent time. Most developmental psychologists, including myself, believe that such periods exist, and we expect that eventually they will be documented by research. We have this conviction partly because we know that the sequence of development is orderly. Children form close emotional bonds to caretakers before they form such bonds to peers. Receptive language must precede productive speech. It is most unusual for a child to learn to read or write if he does not already speak and comprehend speech. Children must be able to stand and talk before they can skip, hop, or dance.

Our belief in sensitive periods persists despite our well-documented conviction that the timing of development is less predictable than the sequences. Eye-hand coordination proceeds rapidly in one infant, slowly in another. This may well imply that the two infants differ in their "sensitive period" for sensory-motor inputs to the development of this coordination. The one child may gain most from such inputs during the second and third months while the other gains most during the fourth and fifth months. Yet a third child might make best use of the same inputs during the fifth and sixth months. In other words, there may be a sensitive or critical period for each child, but its place on an individual's calendar is different. This raises difficulties for the orderly experimenter. Probably the onset of a sensitive period is signalled not by the clock but by the child's behavior. By what he does he tells us that he is ready for new learning. Here we see the link between the psychobiological concept of critical periods and the educational concept of readiness.

Yet another reason that we may have failed to identify critical periods in the preschool years, middle childhood, and adolescence is that we cannot yet say with assurance which inputs are most helpful or most baneful at a given level in a child's development. Some of the inputs that seemed important to one generation of theorists have not held up in research. For example, in the 1940s and the 1950s weaning and toilet training were thought to be critical events in the child's advance toward mastery and self-reliance. Developmental psychologists and anthropologists talked about early and late weaning and toilet training, about abrupt and gradual training approaches, and about harsh and mild methods of inducing the child to give up one set of habits in favor of another. Their research approaches tried to capture the synchrony between the child's readiness and the adult's interventions and also the qualitative nature of those interventions. Caldwell reviewed the extensive literature on these topics in 1964 and left most of us believing that neither a child's experiences with weaning nor his or her experiences with toilet training have predictable long-term effects. We would be more confident of that conclusion if the data did not rely so heavily on retrospective self-report, but even with this source of noise in the data it seems clear that these caretaking interactions are not the critical ones.

Where does this leave the institutions that serve children? Can the notion of critical periods guide their efforts and order their priorities? Can we improve our schools, our neighborhood groups, our health care system, our day care centers, and other institutions serving children by setting their priorities in terms of the putative critical periods through which their clients are passing developmentally? I rather doubt it. As I have mentioned, the evidence concerning infancy is the clearest, so when it comes to social institutions serving infants—of which the family is by all odds the most important—we can draw some guidelines from research. What about other children?

Perhaps the best inference from our present knowledge is that all of childhood is a critical period in life. We need to examine what is being done to support children in general—in contrast with the social and institutional supports for young adults, mature adults, and the elderly and aging—to see whether our priorities match the significance of the entire period of immaturity.

Recently a popular writer published an article in a widely read magazine concerning a program which intervenes in the lives of children during months 8 to 18. The article was enthusiastic in support of the claim that this 10-month period is critical in the child's emotional and cognitive development and, thus, an optimal time for constructive interventions. Professor Edward Zigler of Yale, who was the nation's first Director of our Office of Child Development and who is one of my most distinguished and productive colleagues in developmental psychology, was moved to write to the magazine to say:

> I, for one, am tired of the past decade's scramble to discover some magic period during which interventions will have particu-

larly great payoffs. Some experts emphasize the nine months *in utero;* . . . the period between 8 and 18 months; others, the entire preschool period; and yet others emphasize adolescence. My own predeliction is that we cease this pointless search for magic periods and adopt instead the view that the development process is a continuous one, in which every segment of the life cycle from conception through maturity is of critical importance and requires certain environmental nutrients. (Zigler, 1976, p. 42)

I agree with Dr. Zigler's viewpoint. With respect to the intellectual and social development of the child, the notion of critical periods is a heuristic which organizes our teaching, energizes our research, and brings order into clinical observations. It is not a sufficiently robust notion to be used in organizing social programs for children. For that purpose, it is best to consider all of childhood one critical period. This is the most conservative viewpoint with respect to the present status of our knowledge. It is also a viewpoint which jibes with common sense.

If we see all of childhood as a single, continuous critical period, then we are led to ask what our social institutions are doing to nurture children, not only intellectually, but also socially and emotionally throughout childhood. We are led to compare the social investment being made in children with the investment in other groups such as veterans of wars, the elderly, or the handicapped. We are led to evaluate social practices in terms of their impact on children and families. We will see many handicapping conditions in adulthood as the result of a deprived or distorted childhood, and this view will lead us to emphasize prevention in childhood rather than custodial care of adults.

The notion that a given period in childhood is critical has the advantage that it attracts resources and mobilizes energy toward that period. There may be offsetting disadvantages. The notion may lead some to ignore the needs of younger and older children. It may even seduce some into buckpassing. Zigler comments on the same unfortunate tendency to ignore one period because another seems "critical" when he says, "Ignoring the prenatal period or any other time appears to be the natural course of thought in those who must find some critical period to which to confine their intervention efforts" (1976, p. 42).

There is no doubt that infants need attentive, considerate, timely, and consistent mothering. Those who receive it typically blossom socially. We say that they have developed "a sense of trust," using Erikson's term. What is dangerous is the conclusion that *only* infants need mothering. Equally dangerous is the conclusion that once infancy has passed, it is too late for mothering—the damage caused by deprivation cannot be undone. Both conclusions use the notion of critical periods to justify neglect of the child, as a form of buckpassing. The facts may very well be that attentive and individualized caretaking by someone deeply attached to the child is just as essential for toddlers as for infants. And we know from Skeels' pioneering work that children deprived of individualized care during infancy will blossom when they receive it belatedly as toddlers (Skeels, 1966).

The emphasis on critical periods has led to some dangerous over-simplifications in our thinking about social institutions and children. If a 3-year-old is floundering in social-emotional development, there has been a tendency to look into the child's history for the reason, rather than examine his or her current life circumstances. The evidence simply does not support this pessimism.

The analogy from prenatal morphological development to postnatal personality and cognitive development is heuristic. It sets a tone which appeals to medical students and others trained in the biological sciences. This training has prepared them to accept the way of thinking represented by theorizing about psychological critical periods. Perhaps this is one of the bases for the appeal of this theorizing to psychoanalysts, who have striven for years to convey Freud's insights to all branches of the medical profession. Freud's great contribution was to emphasize the significance of infancy and childhood. Ways are needed to convey this emphasis to a profession whose primary clientele are the middle-aged and the elderly, and whose success to date has been greater in finding cures than in fostering prevention.

I must mention briefly an additional problem with the notion of matching critical periods to institutional priorities. Our language provides little support to efforts to subdivide the two decades of immaturity into distinct periods. Although we are not as badly served by our language as are the French, for whom the term "enfant" covers not only infants but also children and adolescents, our language does not convey the distinctions that seem important to developmental psychologists. The term "toddler" is the best we can do for the significant period in development when the former infant is now upright and moving around in his or her world independently rather than submitting to being moved around by others and is also acquiring speech. The term "preschool child," to which we commonly resort, is just as bad; though it is not as cutesy as "toddler," it describes the former toddler by what he or she is not doing rather than by what he or she is doing. And its denotation varies from state to state within the United States, depending on the state laws about when children enter school. When we speak of an "adolescent," we are talking of a person who might be 9 years old or 19, depending on his or her developmental timetable, and certainly not about the "teenager" our listeners may think of when they hear the term. Child psychologists are constantly hampered in their communication with other professional people, including especially lawyers, by the fact that English gives them no suitable terms for the developmental periods they consider distinctive. Worst of all, even the crude and gross distinctions now available in our language are being blurred by the widespread adoption of the term "kid." I am familiar with day care centers at which 1- and 2-year-old "kids" are cared for by other "kids" who are college-age volunteers and paid assistants.

The present status of knowledge about critical periods in development is good news for social institutions serving children and adolescents. Children's development and their behavior depend vitally on what is happening in their lives currently. We need not abandon hope for a child who has missed critical experiences in earlier years, however diligently we must strive to assure growth-promoting experiences in the earliest years. The evidence does not favor the pessimistic view that many defects and failures are beyond remediation. With children's intellectual and social lags, the problem is not usually that we are too late to help and to educate, but rather that we offer too little.

REFERENCES

Bronson, G. Critical periods in human development. *British Journal of Medical Psychology*, 1962, *35*, 127-133.

Caldwell, B. What is the optimal learning environment for the young child? *American Journal of Orthopsychiatry*, 1967, *37*, 8-21.

Caldwell, B. M. The effects of infant care. In M. L. Hoffman & L. W. Hoffman (Eds.), *Review of child development research* (Vol. 1). New York: Russell Sage, 1964.

Caldwell, B. M. The usefulness of the critical period hypothesis in the study of filiative behavior. *Merrill-Palmer Quarterly of Behavior and Development*, 1962, *8*, 229-242.

Erikson, E. H. *Childhood and society*. New York: Norton, 1950.

Erikson, E. H. *Identity: Youth and crisis*. New York: Norton, 1968.

Erikson, E. H. *Life history and the historical moment*. New York: Norton, 1975.

Heras, I. *Separation and reunion behavior of young children in day care centers*. Unpublished Ph.D. dissertation, Department of Psychology, Stanford University, 1976.

Hunt, J. McV. *Intelligence and experience*. New York: Ronald, 1961.

Hunt, J. McV. The psychological basis for using pre-school enrichment as an antidote for cultural deprivation. *Merrill-Palmer Quarterly of Behavior and Development*, 1964, *10*, 209-248.

Klaus, M. H., & Kennell, J. H. Parent-to-infant attachment. In V. C. Vaughan & T. Brazelton (Eds.), *The family—Can it be saved?* Chicago: Year Book Medical Publishers, 1976.

Klaus, M. H., Leger, T., & Trause, M. A. (Eds.). *Maternal attachment and mothering disorders: A round table*. New Brunswick, N. J.: Johnson and Johnson, 1975.

Lavatelli, C. S. A Piaget-derived model for compensatory pre-school education. In J. L. Frost (Ed.), *Early childhood education rediscovered*. New York: Holt, Rinehart & Winston, 1968.

Lenneberg, E. H. The biological foundations of language. *Hospital Practice*, 1967, *2*, 59-67. Reprinted in T. D. Spencer & N. Kass (Eds.), *Perspectives in child psychology: Research and review*. New York: McGraw-Hill, 1970.

Levinson, G. *Ecology of development: Environmental forces in the everyday lives of the same children in two different milieus*. Dissertation research in progress. Stanford University, 1977.

Lewin, K. *A dynamic theory of personality*. New York: McGraw-Hill, 1935.

Lorenz, K. Der kumpan in der umwelt des vogels. *Journal of Ornithology*, 1935, *83*, 137-213.

Mech, E. V. *Adoption: A policy perspective.* In B. M. Caldwell & H. N. Ricciuti (Eds.), *Review of child development research* (Vol. 3). Chicago: University of Chicago Press, 1973.

Mischel, W. *Personality and assessment.* New York: Wiley, 1968.

Money, J., & Ehrhardt, A. E. *Man and woman, boy and girl.* Baltimore: Johns Hopkins University Press, 1972.

Piaget, J. *The origins of intelligence in children.* New York: International Universities Press, 1952.

Piaget, J. Piaget's theory. In P. H. Mussen (Ed.), *Carmichael's manual of child psychology* (3rd ed.). New York: Wiley, 1970.

Siegel, A. E. Current issues in research on early development. *Human Development,* 1969, *12,* 86-92.

Siegel, A. E. Editorial. *Child Development,* 1967, *38,* 901-907.

Siegel, A. E. Educating females and males to be alive and well in century twenty-one. In M. C. Wittrock (Ed.), *Changing education.* Englewood Cliffs, N.J.: Prentice-Hall, 1973.

Skeels, H. M. Adult status of children with contrasting early life experiences. *Monographs of the Society for Research in Child Development,* 1966, *31* (3, Serial No. 105).

Skeels, H. M. Effects of adoption on children from institutions. *Children,* 1965, *12,* 33-34. Reprinted in J. L. Frost (Ed.), *Early childhood education rediscovered.* New York: Holt, Rinehart & Winston, 1968.

Stendler, C. B. Critical periods in socialization and overdependency. *Child Development,* 1952, *23,* 3-12.

Thompson, W. R., & Grusec, J. E. Studies of early experience. In P. H. Mussen (Ed.), *Carmichael's manual of child psychology* (3rd ed., Vol. 1). New York: Wiley, 1970.

Vaughan, V. C., & Brazelton, T. B. (Eds.). *The family—Can it be saved?* Chicago: Year Book Medical Publishers, 1976.

Volkmar, F. R., & Siegel, A. E. Young children's responses to discrepant social communications. Paper presented at the meeting of the American Psychological Association, Washington, D. C., September 1976.

White, B. L. *The first three years of life.* Englewood Cliffs, N.J.: Prentice-Hall, 1975.

Zigler, E. Filling the preschool gap. Letter to the *New York Times Magazine,* January 18, 1976.

CHANGES IN EVALUATION METHODS

BENJAMIN S. BLOOM
Distinguished Service Professor of Education
University of Chicago

Although educational measurement has existed in some form or other for several thousand years, much of its development into a complex art and technology has taken place during the 20th century. During much of this century, the field has been dominated by the ideas of psychologists, psychometricians, and statisticians. It is only within the past few decades that educational evaluation has sought to free itself from these ancillary fields in order to find clearer roots in the educational process and educational concerns and problems.

Psychological and educational measurement was primarily concerned with the development and utilization of instruments that could be used for prediction, selection, and certification in relation to students and student achievement. Such functions could be served by specialists far removed from education and educational processes in the schools. And, in fact, most of the educational measurement specialists were trained in psychology and statistics with little grounding in the field of education or even educational psychology.

The more recent field of educational evaluation, which was created by Ralph Tyler in the 1930s, has attempted to make use of the precision, objectivity, and mathematical rigor of the psychological measurement field but, in addition, has sought to find ways in which instrumentation and data utilization could more directly be related to educational institutions, educational processes, and educational purposes. In this paper, I will attempt to sketch some of the major dimensions of this work as they appear at this time. I am confident that this field will develop in many new ways and that we can only dimly perceive a few of the major lines this work will take in the future.

EDUCATIONAL PURPOSE AND EDUCATIONAL EVALUATION

Educational purposes, goals, and objectives have been with us since the beginning of formal education. Expressed in verbal form, these statements of intentions were useful in giving a general direction to the educational institution, but only rarely were they operational statements which guided either the teacher or the learner.

In sharp contrast, the instruments for educational measurement (external examinations, teachers' tests and final examinations, standardized tests, etc.) have always had a controlling force on what was taught and, even more, on what was learned by students. Since the major rewards and penalties of an educational system are tied to its certification and grading procedures, which in turn are dependent on its examination procedures, the teaching-learning activities of teachers and students are to a large extent guided by what they expect will be tested on these examinations. And in countries throughout the world, the examination procedures have been largely limited to a single objective—the testing of recall of specific information about each school subject.

Perhaps the major innovation of educational evaluation was the development of ways in which the evaluation process could be integrally related to the educational purposes of the classroom, the school, and the educational system. Much progress in this work has been documented in the many books on educational evaluation, taxonomies of educational objectives, and curriculum evaluation. While there are many differing views about how the objectives should be defined, who has responsibility for determining the objectives, and the precise procedures for evaluating each objective, there is much consensus throughout the world on the importance of relating educational evaluation to educational purposes.

Starting with the pioneering work of Ralph Tyler in the 1930s, the development of evaluation procedures for specific types of educational objectives has moved with careful research and experimentation until it has reached the stage of what might be termed a technology. While there are still many opportunities for creativity and artistry in the construction and use of evaluation procedures, the models and techniques for developing evaluation procedures for major classes of cognitive and affective objectives have been specified in relatively clear detail. Having been involved in this work for over three decades, I have been surprised and delighted to find that most of my students can develop the necessary skills for this work in 3 to 6 months in contrast to the several years necessary to develop similar skills in the 1940s. I attribute much of this to the fact that the procedures are now more clearly developed and illustrated in the many books and manuals on educational evaluation.

It is now common practice for all the major educational testing organizations to start the construction of a new educational test with a detailed set of specifications of the content and objectives to be tested and then to check the validity of the test items against the detailed specifications. Similarly, every new curriculum, research project, or evaluation program starts with the specifications to be met in terms of content and objectives and then develops instruments, sampling procedures, a research design, and data analysis in terms of these specifications. The point is that the linkages between educational purposes and educational research or practice start with this almost as the first step in their work. Also, the detailed procedures for making the linkages are so well developed that evaluation workers can be trained to do it well in much less time than was true several decades earlier.

EDUCATIONAL EVALUATION AS MODELS
FOR TEACHING AND LEARNING

One of the consequences of the linkage between educational purpose and educational evaluation is that the evaluation procedures become operational definitions of educational purposes. It is now possible to classify the items, problems, and procedures being used in examinations, tests, questionnaires, observational forms, and other evaluation material and techniques to determine what purposes are being represented by the evaluation techniques. Thus, in the work of the International Studies of Educational Achievement (IEA) (Carroll, 1976; Comber & Keeves, 1973;

Foshay, 1962; Husén, 1967; Lewis & Massad, 1975; Purves, 1973; Thorndike, 1973; Torney, Oppenheim, & Farnen, 1976), a collection of the evaluation procedures being used within a nation, when properly analyzed, give more operational information about the educational objectives of a school subject or curriculum than do the verbal statements about the course or curriculum (Bloom, 1974a).

Furthermore, the actual materials of instruction and the observations of teaching-learning situations can be analyzed to determine the appropriate evaluation procedures and, in turn, the relation between the stated objectives and the learning experiences available to students. The evaluation procedures then can be determined in great detail. From these analyses, one can get a better picture of the kinds of learning being developed in a classroom, school, or entire educational system than is likely to be true from observations that might take several years to carry out. These analyses of "the opportunity to learn" have been very effective in predicting (and accounting for) the kinds of learning eventually found on major national or international survey instruments such as those reported in the IEA studies.

There are, however, even more important consequences of the linkage between educational purpose and educational evaluation. One can determine where the linkages are distorted between educational purposes, instruction, and evaluation. Is it that the purposes are beyond the present capabilities of the evaluators to develop appropriate evaluation procedures? If so, then the task of training educational evaluators to construct more valid and appropriate evaluation procedures becomes clear. Is it that the teachers have not yet learned how to provide instruction for particular educational purposes? If so, then the need for preservice and inservice education of teachers becomes clear. If the task of providing such training appears insurmountable for economic reasons or because of the present capabilities and training of the teaching staff, then can the situation be remedied by improvements in the instructional materials; by the use of radio, TV, or educational films; or by the use of peer tutoring and other special instructional procedures?

It is evident that students attempt to learn the skills, abilities, and subject content that they believe will be emphasized in the evaluation procedures they will be judged on. If they believe this is largely rote information, they will study and prepare accordingly. If they believe they will be judged on their ability to use the ideas and processes in new situations, they will learn and prepare to demonstrate such abilities. There has been a great deal of observational studies, as well as more direct experimental research, on how students learn and prepare in relation to different kinds of examinations. The evidence is unmistakable: Students will attempt to learn what they anticipate will be emphasized in the evaluation instruments on which they expect to be judged, graded, and certified. There is little doubt that a series of major changes in the evaluation procedures over a number of years can bring about great changes in the learning of the students—probably more change than could be produced by any other single change in the educational situation. This is, of course, a two-edged sword in that negative changes (reduction in the quality of learning) as well as positive changes (improvements in the quality of learning) can be produced by related changes in the evaluation procedures. But the point of this relation between student learning and evaluation is that the evaluation procedures furnish *models* of what learning is expected and the models are clearer than the more ambiguous statements of educational purposes or the complex range of instructional materials and procedures to which the students have been exposed. The clearest guide that students have as to what learning (largely cognitive) is expected of them is the evaluation instruments on which they will be judged and graded.

Similarly, teachers are also guided by the evaluation procedures as to what they are to teach and what will be expected of their students. Even when the evaluation procedures are made by the teachers themselves, they define the end learning products of their own teaching and they strive to prepare their students to do well on these evaluation instruments. If the evaluation procedures largely deal with rote types of learning, teachers will prepare their students for such types of evaluation. If the evaluation procedures largely deal with application of ideas to new problems, then teachers will attempt to develop these kinds of learning in their students. It has been found that one of the most effective ways of preparing teachers to teach higher mental processes is to develop skills for testing such processes in the teachers and to help them include problems of the appropriate type in their own evaluation procedures.

EVALUATION AS AN INTEGRAL PART OF INSTRUCTION AND LEARNING

Evaluation instruments do serve as models for teaching and learning and, as such, help to guide both instruction and student learning. Evaluation used this way is largely a perceptual phenomenon in that teachers and students have expectations as to the evaluation procedures to be used (sometimes incorrect), and their efforts are guided by these expectations. Thus, the evaluation procedures serve to indicate the goals to be reached at the end of some period of instruction and learning.

Many of us have searched for ways in which evaluation might become a more integral part of the process of teaching and learning during the actual process. We had become aware of the effects of the frequency of testing on the learning of students (typically the more frequent the testing the higher the achievement); the ways in which some teachers analyze the results of their progress tests and quizzes to determine wherein they should stress certain points, review others, and even provide special help for students who have difficulties; and the effects of the kind of testing and the frequency of testing on the preparation that students make as well as the pacing of their learning activities. In addition, we became aware of the effects of group instruction on the differential learning of students within a class.

Much of the research on classroom instruction has demonstrated that students differ in their learning even though theoretically all had equal opportunity to learn in the same classroom. We conceived of this differential learning as errors in both instruction and learning and we took the position that if errors in student learning are systematically corrected at each stage in the learning process, there should be little variation in the final outcomes as measured by a summative evaluation measure. Furthermore, students who are corrected at each stage of learning should achieve at a much higher level than other students who have not been helped when they needed it, even though both groups of students are in the same classroom or are taught similarly by the same teacher.

This systematic corrective learning has been termed mastery learning and there are a number of teaching strategies to achieve such mastery. Central to most mastery learning strategies is the use of *feedback* and *corrective* procedures at various stages or parts of the learning process. While a variety of feedback processes are possible (including quizzes, homework, workbooks, etc.), it has been found that the development and use of brief diagnostic tests have proven to be most effective. Such diagnostic or formative tests are intended to determine what *each* learner has learned in a particular unit, chapter, or part of the course and what he or she still needs to learn. In general, these formative tests are not used to grade or judge the student and their main value is in providing feedback to both teachers and students on the particular aspects or elements of the learning unit that still need to be mastered. The effectiveness of mastery learning work is clearly related to the degree of efficiency of formative tests in pinpointing the learning needs of each student.

The key to the success of mastery learning strategies, however, largely lies in the extent to which students can be motivated and helped to correct their learning difficulties at the appropriate points in the learning process. Many teachers have been very effective in motivating students to do the necessary additional work and in finding ways of providing the correctives they need. The research done so far in the United States, Canada, South Korea, and a number of other countries suggests that the development of a student partner system or providing opportunities for groups of two or three students to work together are very effective methods of motivating each student to do corrective work, and, in addition, this provides the additional time and help a student may need. Teacher aides, programmed instruction, audio tapes or cassettes, and other instructional material appear to work well in particular situations. In most situations, the corrective work following the formative test feedback is done outside of the regular classroom time.

In the many studies reported by Block (1971, 1974) and by Peterson (1972), there is considerable evidence that mastery learning procedures do work well in enabling about 80 percent of the students to reach a level of achievement which less than 20 percent of the students attain under nonmastery or conventional teaching methods. The time costs for the mastery learning is typically of the order of 10 to 20 percent additional time over the classroom scheduled time for those students who need it. In a number of studies, it has been found that the extra time and help needed steadily decreases and toward the end of the course, little or no corrective work is needed to attain the criterion of mastery on the formative tests (Bloom 1974b).

While there are many different approaches to the improvement of both instruction and learning through mastery, the effectiveness of most of these approaches is dependent on the use of feedback and corrective procedures. Evaluation plays a central role in providing the feedback on the effects of instruction as well as on the effectiveness of the correction procedures. Properly used, the evaluation is looked upon by both teachers and learners as an indispensable tool for instruction and learning, especially when the formative evaluation is not used to grade or judge either the teacher or the student.

Many countries have been experimenting with different mastery learning strategies. Typically, they are finding that after the formative tests and corrective procedures are developed by evaluation and curriculum specialists, the costs of mastery learning are negligible. Furthermore, they are finding that the outcomes in terms of final achievement, student attitudes toward learning, and improvement in student general ability to learn under school conditions are so great as to represent positive human development in its own right as well as economic benefits that are far greater than might be expected from the time or other costs incurred.

However, for the purposes of this paper, the main point to be stressed is that the use of evaluation as an integral part of instruction and learning has enormous consequences. We must continue to search for additional effective ways in which evaluation can contribute to the teaching-learning process as an integral part of that process.

EVALUATION TO DETERMINE THE EFFECTIVENESS
OF INSTRUCTION AND LEARNING

Much of the use of evaluation has been to determine the learning outcomes of particular types of curriculum and instruction. Typically, the attempt is made to construct evaluation procedures that are appropriate to a particular educational program, curriculum, or instructional approach. Then, an appropriate research design and a sampling procedure are chosen to determine whether in fact the educational program, course, etc., did have specific traceable effects on student learning.

Rarely does an educational system restrict itself to a single educational program, curriculum, or instructional approach for all students of a particular age or grade. Evaluation is useful in determining the relative effectiveness of the different approaches to instruction and learning. Evaluation used this way has characteristically been used to determine whether alternative A is, in terms of student learning, more effective than alternatives B, C, D, etc. (alternatives may be programs, courses, curricula, teaching methods, class size, instructional strategies, etc.). In most of the research using this evaluation approach, it has characteristically been found that the "opportunity to learn" particular content and objectives in a particular alternative is highly related to the evaluation results for that alternative. That is, if students are taught x, y, and z they tend to learn x, y, and z, while if they are taught only x and z they learn accordingly. This seems so obvious that one wonders why evaluation is necessary.

However, there are great discrepancies between what an educational program is *intended* to accomplish, what students are *actually given an opportunity to learn*, and what *students actually learn*; and the discrepancies have to do with what happens in particular classrooms (opportunity to learn) in relation to what was intended and the evaluation results. Thus, the basic problem of the effects of an educational alternative is dependent on the linkages between the intended effects of a program, what happens in the school or classroom, and the evaluation results. If an educational program is designed to produce a particular set of results, we must insure that the appropriate use of the program actually takes place in the classroom before we can be certain that we are really evaluating the effectiveness of the program. In response to this problem, educational evaluators and researchers now seek to establish what actually takes place in the classrooms they evaluate before claiming they are evaluating the effectiveness of the specific program. Increasingly, evaluators are selecting classrooms and teachers where they are certain that the program is actually being implemented in the intended ways before applying their evaluation procedures.

Once they can satisfy themselves that the classrooms or teachers are fully implementing the intended curriculum, program, or method, they can determine its effectiveness as well as its difficulties. Then, the research moves to the problems of how the program can be fully implemented in other classrooms—training of teachers, orientation of students, appropriate materials, or the supporting conditions of morale, educational leadership, supervisors, consultants, etc., that are necessary for its full implementation with other teachers and classrooms.

Perhaps the main lesson to be learned from the attempts to evaluate new early childhood educational programs (Headstart), new programs for the disadvantaged students (compensatory education), programmed instruction, new curricula (new mathematics, new biology, etc.), and new teaching strategies is that there are great gaps between the intended new program and its full realization in the classrooms. In fact, one has to search very carefully before finding the few classrooms where the new program is fully realized. Policymakers who sponsor and give economic support to the new educational alternatives must be aware that good intentions (especially new ones) are not enough in education. The problems of how the good intentions can be fully implemented in the classroom must be solved before the new program can be evaluated.

Closely related to the foregoing points is the increasing use of evaluation to determine how an alternative can be modified and improved. New approaches to education are rarely perfect and seldom are they universal panaceas. At one time, evaluation was used primarily to determine whether alternative A was better than B, or C. It mattered little that the statistical significance of the difference between the alternatives was rarely matched by the educational or social significance of the differences. Now, however, evaluation increasingly is being used not only to determine which alternatives are superior, but also how they can be further improved. A new curriculum or program may be excellent in terms of certain characteristics but should be modified in terms of other characteristics. When the evaluation and other data are properly analyzed, they reveal what is excellent about an educational alternative, what is good but could be improved, and what is poor and needs much further work.

For the educational policymaker or administrator, the basic point is that major changes in programs should be instituted only when there is clear evidence that a particular existing program is poor in all respects. Improvements and modifications in existing programs may be more effective than the creation of entirely new programs. Smaller changes cause less dislocation in the schools and may, under appropriate conditions, be more effective in promoting improved instruction and student learning than will completely new programs. It is likely that the enormous expenditure of resources (economic as well as human) of introducing great changes in teachers, materials, and educational points of view will be cost effective only when all aspects of the new program are working effectively in the classrooms and school.

A final point to be made on evaluation and effectiveness of instruction and learning is that times and conditions change. An educational program that is very effective at one time may in a number of years become less effective. A new curriculum which works superbly in year x may in year x + 5 work very poorly. The deterioration of particular new programs, curricula, and teaching methods has been well documented, especially in relation to some of the major educational changes introduced during the past decade in the U. S. as well as other countries.

Increasingly, educational evaluation is seen as a quality control measure. That is, carefully selected samples of students, classrooms, and schools are surveyed at particular times to determine whether a new program that worked well at one time still continues to work well or to determine whether particular aspects of the program need to be modified at particular points in time if the program is to continue to work well in the classrooms. Sometimes, it is found that the program continues to be effective with some students and some teachers or schools but works less well in certain respects with other students and teachers. Again, the point is that the educational policymakers or administrator must not expect that education can be a fixed and static thing. Times and conditions change and evaluation can reveal when and where the changes require modification and improvements in the educational programs.

EDUCATIONAL EVALUATION AND EDUCATION

Education in Western societies is frequently equated with schooling. We support schools to give our children and youth an education. We empower schools to give formal recognition to the amount and type of education an individual has completed by the use of credits, certificates, and academic degrees. Most of our writing and research on education deal only with schools and schooling.

This equation of education and schooling has been attacked by scholars of education as well as by more radical reformers who insist that much learning can and does take place outside the school. But equally important, research on education and research on various aspects of the society have questioned some of the relations between the school system and other subsystems in the society.

Research into the relationship between the schools and the home environment has been one of the more fruitful areas of study stimulated by these questions. Home is a powerful educational environment, especially during the preschool and primary school years. Studies of home environments in the United States as well as in several other countries reveal the effect of the home on language development, ability to learn from adults, attitudes toward school learning, and aspirations for further education and the occupational careers and life styles associated with education. It is clear that when the home and the school have congruent learning emphases, the child has little difficulty in his later schooling. But when the home and the school have very divergent approaches to life and to learning, the child is likely to be penalized severely by the school, especially when school attendance is required for 10 or more years.

During the past decade, we have begun to recognize some of the problems raised by disparities between home and school. One approach has been to preempt some of the years preceding regular school by placing children in preschool programs. Other attempts have been made to alter some aspects of the primary school. Still other efforts have been made to alter the home environment. There is no doubt that these attempts to alter the relations between home and school have raised many problems. The resolution of these problems and the appropriate relations between home and school will concern us for many years to come.

Schools and peer groups are increasingly in conflict, and the individual appears to learn very different things in these two subsystems of society. Especially during adolescence do we find these two subsystems diverging. The conflicts between the values emphasized by schools and colleges and the values emphasized by various peer groups raise serious questions about the ways in which these two sets of values can be more effectively related. What we desperately need are research and scholarship that will point the way to the resolution of some of the more disturbing conflicts between the schools and adolescent peer groups.

Recent research by economists attempts to understand the relationships between the economic system of a nation and its educational system. It is evident that the relations between education and economics may be very different for societies at different stages of industrialization as well as for societies that have very different political systems. The view that education can be conceived of as investment in human capital has stimulated educators as well as economists to study the economic effects of different approaches to education. The view of education as both a consumer or cultural good and an investment in human capital alters many of our traditional views about education and its effects. This area of research raises long-term problems about the consequences of this view for support of the schools and support of students in the schools.

There are other subsystems in a nation—religion, mass media, the political system, the status system—that have very complex relations with education. Perhaps the main point is that education is not confined to the school system and that very complex educational and other relations are found between the schools as a subsystem and the other subsystems within a society. While we have tended to think of a system of schooling as relatively insulated from other parts of the society, it is likely that the schools will be under pressure to relate more clearly to the other parts of the social system. Undoubtedly, we will come to regard education during the school-attending period (as well as before and after this period) as most appropriately the concern of many aspects of the society. Increasingly we will try to determine what can best be learned in the schools, what can best be learned elsewhere, and what can be learned only through an effective interrelation of different parts of the social system.

Evaluation methods are gradually being developed to appraise the learning of a population both in the school as well as outside of the school. The new ideas on national assessment that are being developed in a number of countries are efforts to determine what has been learned in the schools, what has been learned elsewhere, and what has been learned in the interaction between the schools and other subsystems in a nation. This work is of recent development and it will be some time before evaluators are effective in determining both the extent of the learning as well as the source.

Once again, the point is that education and educational policymakers must learn to use evaluation and evaluation data to secure a broader picture of the educational resources of a nation than may be secured from viewing the schools as the single educational resource. This is probably the most complex problem that educational evaluators and policymakers must face. The challenges faced by these broader issues suggest that international seminars and conferences may be necessary if the problems and progress of various national attempts in this field are to be studied and utilized where relevant by other national groups.

Educational evaluation may contribute to the improvement of education in many countries of the world. The enormous resources being expended in each country for education makes it mandatory that some forms of educational evaluation be used for appraising the effectiveness of particular aspects of a national educational program, for determining where it is in need of modification or major changes, and for determining how to maintain and even improve the effectiveness of the schools as well as the related educational resources of the nation.

The appropriate training of highly competent educational evaluation specialists is a minimum requirement if effective use is to be made of this rapidly developing technology. The support of and the appropriate relations between such specialists, educational policymakers, and the educational institutions of a nation are necessary to maintain educational evaluation at a high level and to insure that the evaluation methods and results play their appropriate role in the continued maintenance and improvement of complex educational systems.

REFERENCES

Block, J. H. (Ed.). *Mastery learning: Theory and practice.* New York: Holt, Rinehart & Winston, 1971.

Block, J. H. (Ed.). *Schools, society, and mastery learning.* New York: Holt, Rinehart & Winston, 1974.

Bloom, B. S. Implications of the IEA studies for curriculum and instruction. *School Review,* 1974, *82,* 413-435. (a)

Bloom, B. S. Time and learning. *American Psychologist,* 1974, *29,* 682-688. (b)

Carroll, J. B. *French as a foreign language in eight countries: International studies in evaluation V.* New York: Wiley, 1976.

Comber, L. C., & Keeves, J. P. *Science education in nineteen countries: International studies in evaluation I.* New York: Wiley, 1973.

Foshay, A. W. (Ed.), *Educational achievements of 13-year-olds in twelve countries.* Hamburg: UNESCO Institute for Education, 1962.

Husén, T. (Ed.), *International study of achievement in mathematics: A comparison of twelve countries* (2 vols.). New York: Wiley, 1967.

Lewis, E. G., & Massad, C. E. *English as a foreign language in ten countries: International studies in evaluation IV*. New York: Wiley, 1975.

Peterson, P. *A review of the research on mastery learning strategies.* Unpublished manuscript, International Association for the Evaluation of Educational Achievement, 1972. (Also available from Stanford Center for Research and Development in Teaching, Stanford, California.)

Purves, A. C. *Literature education in ten countries: International studies in evaluation II*. New York: Wiley, 1973.

Thorndike, R. L. *Reading comprehension education in fifteen countries: International studies in evaluation III*. New York: Wiley, 1973.

Torney, J. V., Oppenheim, A. N., & Farnen, R. F. *Civic education in ten countries: International studies in evaluation VI*. New York: Wiley, 1976.

EDUCATIONAL RESEARCH AND DEVELOPMENT:
PAST AND FUTURE

ROBERT M. GAGNÉ
Professor of Instructional Design and Development
Florida State University

It has now been 20 years since the federal government undertook to have centrally planned and managed programs of educational research and development. This period began with the passage and implementation of the Cooperative Research Program in 1954 and has continued through a period of establishment of regional laboratories and research centers to the present set of programs brought together under the National Institute of Education.

There are surely people at this symposium who have followed these developments more closely, and who are aware of their vicissitudes much more intimately than I am. Except for three or four relatively brief periods of fairly direct involvement in the planning of the inner workings of several different parts of this national program, I have remained an "outside" observer. Perhaps I should say, incidentally, that those involvements I did have with the national program aroused some degree of fright, mixed with anger, for reasons that you can readily imagine. But I mention these things mainly to establish my credibility as a "distant" rather than an "involved" observer.

Has a national program of educational research and development done any good? Has it accomplished something over this 20-year period? On the whole, I think it has accomplished several things, and, not surprisingly perhaps, left some things still to be done. Let me say a few words about what seems to have been done in several functional areas.

BASIC RESEARCH

What has happened to basic research as a result of these national programs? The initial impact of the Cooperative Research Program, it seems to me, was fairly successful in attracting and converting the interests of investigators to problems derived from education. This program, through its funding of field-initiated research, attracted a number of people from the basic disciplines of psychology, anthropology, economics, and other sciences, some of whom remained converted to seeking their problems in this area. When the Cooperative Research Program ended or was weakened by being scattered into various applied subprograms, some of these investigators reverted to their previous pursuits. Some remained interested in education, and they can probably be counted on the fingers of a few hands.

Meanwhile, the opportunities for pursuing basic research derived from educational problems came to be concentrated increasingly in a few university-based centers. Outstanding examples of basic research production have come from the Wisconsin Center and the Learning Research and Development Center (LRDC) at Pittsburgh. The productiveness of LRDC in basic research, as well as in related applied research, has been truly remarkable and admirable over the period of its existence. Those of us who serve on its Board of Visitors know well how exciting it is to receive reports and reprints of excellent research on important basic problems of education.

Thus, at the present time, it appears that basic research relevant to education is being carried on in exemplary fashion to a large degree by a few research and development centers. With the proper kind of leadership, the research and development center seems to be an excellent way to get important research done. However, it is also apparent, I think, that the output of basic research by university centers is limited not only in amount but also in scope. Viewing the national scene as a whole, it appears to me that the "barrel" of knowledge is being served by only a few spigots. The barrel, if that is what it is, is not very full. In the current climate of concern for such aspects of research and development as evaluation and dissemination and given the general tightness of federal funding, some attention needed to be paid to this problem, at least from a long-range point of view.

DEVELOPMENT

As for development of educational products and procedures, this indeed has had a checkered history. Many actors have been on this stage, including the Office of Education, the National Institute of Education, the National Science Foundation, private foundations, and commercial publishers. It is indeed a difficult area for national planning, and apparently many mistakes have been made. Surely, many educational materials have been developed that have never been used or used only in single classrooms. One suspects, too, that many expensive educational materials were developed that never should have been used because their effects were not properly evaluated.

My impression is that the fundamental problem of development of educational materials and procedures has not been solved. The problem is that since there are so many variables affecting educational outcomes, optimizing one of them often cannot have the expected effects unless others are optimized at the same time. Introducing to schools a new set of materials in math, or science, or reading, does not have a beneficial effect unless relevant teaching procedures, teacher assignment policies, organizational factors, and a number of other variables are also optimized. Can all these things be changed at once? Perhaps so, and perhaps it is true that some individual schools have managed to do just that. But if this is so, obviously the problem of "development" is a large one, not to be solved solely by efforts to develop new and up-to-date materials.

More new materials, optimized in their development, or for that matter, more new instructional procedures do not appear in themselves to be accomplishing the end of improving educational outcomes. In the workaday school, it is my strong impression that varieties of new materials may often work against educational improvement because their very numbers and varieties are confusing to teachers. Nowhere is this more apparent than in the field of reading. In that field, the materials available have been developed from several different and conflicting sets of principles. Their existence tends to create and to perpetuate the notion that each child learns to read in a different way. In one sense, this statement is a profound truth; but in another practical sense, it is profound rubbish. Meanwhile, children who need to learn to read and are quite capable of it, are not learning to do so. Surely the situation is one that raises the question as to how development of educational products and prcedures should be done to achieve the best ultimate results.

At any rate, over this period of 20 years, the national program has stimulated many educational developments. At the level of local schools, the regional laboratories and centers have cooperatively developed many individual materials and procedures, presumably adapted to local needs. There are programs in reading and mathematics from the Wisconsin Center, programs in early reading and language development from the Southwestern Regional Laboratory, and (not least) IPI (Individually Prescribed Instruction) materials from the Learning Research and Development Center and Research for Better Schools, among many others.

Are these various developed products better than others; for example, better than those that might be developed by commercial sources, or possibly by nationally funded curriculum projects? The answer to this question is hard to come by. However, it seems to me that agencies funded by the national education program have made substantial contributions, and that they cannot be said to have been unworthy efforts, considered as a whole. In particular, these developmental efforts have been distinguished by their championship of the principle of *empirical validation*, in the form of formative and summative evaluation. This principle has influenced many other developments, including those that are sponsored by commercial publishers and even those supported by other national agencies. Surely this trend toward product evaluation is a positive one that will not readily be diminished in the future.

EVALUATION

In the field of evaluation itself, many contributions have been made by centers, laboratories, and other organizations funded by national programs. There has, of course, been a surge of concern over the question of what makes a difference—do teachers make a difference, do materials make a difference, do methods make a difference? The whole area of effort has undergone an expansion in scope, partly in recognition of the fact that evaluation, if it is to be effective, must be planned from the very beginning of a program. Equally important, perhaps, has been the recognition that evaluation does not equate simply to the assessment of student achievement, even though that still remains a critical output measure. Evaluators have found that they must be concerned also with (1) the nature of the student input, (2) the so-called *process* measures of what happens in the delivery of the content to be learned, as well as (3) the product as indicated by changes in student performance.

As I have mentioned, there have been many contributors to the development of evaluation technology. I believe that at least two highly important contributions have been made by LRDC. The first is the concept of criterion-referenced testing, described briefly by Glaser in his *American Psychologist* article (1963), and more extensively by Glaser and Klaus (1961), and again by Glaser and Nitko (1971). There has subsequently been a great deal of writing by others on this concept, some of which sounds like hand-wringing on the part of those who are schooled in traditional test theory. I would define this concept of test design as one which states that a carefully defined domain from which test items are selected must be the criterion of test construction. In test development, this domain must remain primary and inviolate, regardless of whatever other characteristics of the test have to be. If particular arrangements have to be made to achieve reliability or difficulty or whatever, these must be made with no compromising of the criterion.

The particular name for this concept, "criterion-referenced," may not remain. Already such tests of student achievement are being called "domain-referenced," "objective-referenced," and other things. Yet the concept itself must prevail, if we are to have rationally sound measures of the outcomes of education. The development of techniques for criterion-referenced testing still has a long way to go. The promise of the Glaser and Klaus (1961) chapter on proficiency assessment has by no means yet been realized. For instance, techniques of criterion-referenced test development now pertain almost exclusively to intellectual skills (like those in mathematics). We do not yet know how to apply this concept to other varieties of outcome, such as knowledge or attitudes. There is still much to be done.

A second contribution to the evaluation field is the model for evaluation proposed by Cooley and his associates (Cooley & Leinhardt, 1975; Cooley & Lohnes, 1976). This also seems to me to be an important accomplishment. This model begins with the assessment of initial student performance as a base against which change is to be measured. It then divides the influencing factors of the educational situation into the categories of opportunity, motivators, content structure, and instructional events. Measures are sought of these factors within each category. And finally, there are assessments of outcomes. The contribution made by this model is the important one of sorting out the classes of influence that may be expected to affect educational outcomes. As is well known, previous studies of "what makes a difference" have experienced particular difficulties in this sorting operation. The proposed model appears to hold much promise as a realistic solution to these difficulties.

These two developments—criterion-referenced testing and a system for identifying and separating the effects of influencing variables—lie at the heart of the evaluation problem. They will require a great deal of further attention in the years to come.

DISSEMINATION

Let me turn to another aspect of the research and development spectrum, one which nowadays is enjoying considerable attention on the part of the national program. This is called "dissemination," or sometimes "diffusion." It has been apparent for quite a long time that many valuable ideas, products, techniques, and procedures, even when they may have considerable supporting evidence for their effectiveness, all too often have a hard time getting adopted and used by schools. Now, of course, there always has been some sort of diffusion process: for example, that provided by the faculty member of the school of education to the student teacher or even directly via inservice education programs to the school itself. But this system simply does not get the job done of conveying practical information to the schools, or instituting and monitoring the process of adoption of new products or procedures. Perhaps it did in an earlier period, but it does not do it today.

My impression is that the national centers, and particularly the laboratories, have been doing a great deal to fill this gap between the development of systematic knowledge and products and their utilization by schools. Of course the example that is close to home is the diffusion of the IPI system by Research for Better Schools. But all of the laboratories have been engaged in diffusion, and they still are. Look, for example, at the list of training programs, workshops, and conferences currently being conducted by the Northwest Regional Laboratory in virtually all parts of the country including Alaska. They are on all sorts of subjects of importance to schools that are instituting new educational programs—on bilingual education, on health education, on career education, on competency-based education, etc. One could no doubt find a very comprehensive list of dissemination and diffusion activities which have been going on for up to 10 years by the laboratories and the centers.

The fact seems to be, however, that all of this effort, valuable though it may be, does not solve the problem of dissemination in any permanent way. For a more long-lasting solution, I believe the studies conducted by the Far West Laboratory (Carlisle, Cone, & Whitney, 1971) will be a source of important information, if they are not already serving this function. A few years ago, this laboratory undertook to study the problem of how new research and development findings, new programs, and new products could find their way to adoption and use by schools. Their finding was, to put it all too briefly, that the whole process of two-way communication between the R&D community and the schools must be institutionalized. The function of dissemination must be identified as a definite job function in the R&D organization and also in the school system and the school itself. I believe this is the kind of answer we are currently groping toward, although progress is still pretty slow.

To summarize, I believe that the national program supporting research and development in education has some substantial accomplishments to its credit. First of all, it has increased the awareness of the role and value of research and development among school boards, school administrators, and teachers. I do not mean to imply that the millenium has arrived, but simply that educational research and development has come out of the closet into the light of increased public awareness. In basic research, much good work has been done, and the level and scope of educationally relevant research activity has definitely increased. Nevertheless, the knowledge base is thin as of today. In development, despite constantly shifting guidelines for program emphasis, the centers and laboratories have developed some valuable and useful products and procedures, which compare favorably with the outcomes of national curriculum efforts of other sponsorship and favorably also with the best of commercially developed products. In evaluation, there have been many developments which have been supported by national programs—in fact, the whole field of evaluation has been greatly enlarged in its scope. In dissemination and diffusion activities, the centers and more particularly the laboratories have appeared to be filling a huge gap that is not otherwise served by educational agencies at the state or national level. Probably some of their work and their experience can even now be put to good use in finding a more lasting solution to the pressing problem of utilization of research and development outcomes.

REFERENCES

Carlisle, D. H., Cone, P. E., & Whitney, B. G. *The instructional planning team: An organizational arrangement to accomplish planning, teaching, and evaluation in a school—A pilot study.* Berkeley, Cal.: Far West Laboratory for Educational Research and Development, 1971.

Cooley, W. W., & Leinhardt, G. *The application of a model for investigating classroom processes.* Pittsburgh: University of Pittsburgh, Learning Research and Development Center, 1975.

Cooley, W. W., & Lohnes, P. R. *Evaluation research in education.* New York: Irvington Publishers, 1976.

Glaser, R. Instructional technology and the measurement of learning outcomes: Some questions. *American Psychologist,* 1963, *18,* 519-521.

Glaser, R., & Klaus, D. J. Proficiency measurement: Assessing human performance. In R. M. Gagné (Ed.), *Psychological principles in systems development.* New York: Holt, Rinehart & Winston, 1961.

Glaser, R., & Nitko, A. J. Measurement in learning and instruction. In R. L. Thorndike (Ed.), *Educational measurement* (2nd ed.). Washington, D. C.: American Council on Education, 1971.

HOW SCHOOLS UTILIZE
EDUCATIONAL RESEARCH AND DEVELOPMENT

RALPH W. TYLER
Director Emeritus
Center for Advanced Study in the Behavioral Sciences
Senior Consultant, Science Research Associates

Seven years ago, while I was Chairman of the Research Advisory Council of the Office of Education, the appropriation voted for educational research and development was markedly below the authorization and the long-range plan. When I talked with the Secretary of HEW, he told me that there was no important legislative constituency pressing for the appropriation; in fact, the school administrators were saying that the schools were getting no significant help from the expanded research program authorized by the Elementary and Secondary Education Act of 1965. Conversations with several members of Congress corroborated the Secretary's comments. At about the same time, Stephen Bailey sent questionnaires to a sample of school administrators, asking about their uses of the products of educational research and development. Their replies cited very few research findings that they were employing in their schools.

Is it true, as is often stated, that the reports of educational research sit on library shelves gathering dust, and that the systems and materials developed as products of research and development efforts are adopted only by a few schools and only for a short time? This point of view is all too commonly held, but I believe that this attitude is largely due to a lack of clear understanding of the research and development enterprise in education and the way in which the school as a social system draws upon knowledge and utilizes new systems and materials. The purpose of this paper is to explore these matters briefly and to suggest some of their implications for the planning and conduct of research and development programs in education.

THE TIME FACTOR

One obvious explanation for the fact that most teachers and administrators do not report that they use the results of educational research in their work is the cumulative nature of systematic knowledge, and, therefore, much of it that we use was formulated in the past. For example, we now take for granted that interest in a learning activity is an important positive factor in a pupil's learning. However, when John Dewey discovered this in his work with his laboratory school in Chicago, it was a new finding contradicting the folklore of education—that learning tasks to be effective must be hard and unpleasant. His little book, *Interest and Effort in Education* (1913), created a debate among professionals for 20 years before the idea became an accepted pedagogical principle. The Department of Defense conducted a study of the sources of knowledge used in designing a modern weapons system and found that more than 80 percent of the research findings used in this project were published 25 or more years before. When new knowledge is incorporated into the common practices of a profession, practitioners rarely know the source of the knowledge and are not likely to appreciate the contribution that earlier research has made to their work.

RESEARCH DISTINGUISHED FROM DEVELOPMENT

The time factor is not the only one that has created misunderstanding. The nature of research and the difference between research and development are not well understood. Research is an activity seeking to gain greater understanding of a phenomenon, while development is an effort to design a system that will achieve desired ends under specified conditions or constraints. There is also evaluative research that compares the realities of the system with the intentions and conditions, specified or implied, in the plans. Often, practitioners do not understand these distinctions and will ask of research such questions as: How can I eliminate disruptive behavior in the classroom? How can we get the school tax levy raised? How can I give instructional leadership in my school? How can I teach disadvantaged children to read?

Research may provide greater understanding of such a problem as disruptive behavior in classrooms by studying instances of it that may lead to the building of a taxonomy of types, identifying kinds of students involved, describing the contexts in which they occur, the antecedent events, and the consequences. But systematic efforts to eliminate or reduce this behavior requires the design of a procedure (development) and the testing of the procedure in practice (evaluative research). Practitioners in most fields have not had much experience in calling upon research, development, and evaluative research in connection with their own work; thus, they have not learned to make these distinctions, nor discovered their usefulness.

THE EVOLUTION OF PROFESSIONAL PRACTICE

Researchers and many academics also misunderstand educational practice. The practice of every profession evolves informally, and professional procedures are not generally derived from a systematic design based on research findings. Professional practice has largely developed through trial and error and intuitive efforts. Practitioners, over the years, discover procedures that appear to work and others that fail. The professional practice of teaching, as well as that of law, medicine, and theology, is largely a product of the experience of practitioners, particularly those who are more creative, inventive, and observant than the average.

Research and development activities furnish a more systematic basis for building a body of practices and an intellectual doctrine, and they can also furnish a basis for dealing with new problems and improving practice. But science explains phenomena, it does not produce practices. Hence, both researcher and developer must turn to the phenomena of learning and teaching in order to derive data for their work. This seems, sometimes, to be forgotten. It is, thus, appropriate in this symposium to try to look at research and development through the eyes of practitioners—teachers and administrators.

CURRENT USES OF RESEARCH

Practitioners do use research. As I review my experiences, going back as far as the Eight-Year Study 40 years ago, in working with teachers, principals, curriculum specialists, school administrators, and others, I can identify two very common uses of research—in the conceptions that make up their "cognitive maps" and in the generalizations that guide the conscious performance of their professional tasks. Everyone employs a "cognitive map," that is, to define it metaphorically, a picture in their mind of the complex phenomena with which they deal. One's map of instruction may be very simple—certain things to be learned, pupils to learn them, and learning activities through which the pupil will learn the desired things. But teachers quickly discover that this map is too simple to help them identify what is wrong when the pupils do not learn even though they go through the activities. They then look for refinements in their maps, additional concepts that help them to understand the phenomena they encounter as teachers, and they will add and modify their maps from time to time as they become aware of new concepts that appear to give greater richness to the representation they have of the situation.

The "cognitive map" of principals is likely to be somewhat different from that of teachers because their map deals with phenomena for which they have responsibility. The principal's map will include such concepts as teachers, their relations with the principal, the principal's role in this relationship and in the activities involved, and the like. The conscious procedures of the different professionals are guided by a map which represents the picture in their minds of the phenomena with which they deal and by generalizations that help them understand their practices.

Obviously, concepts and generalizations differ not only in their degree of complexity but also in their consistency with relevant reality. The validity and adequacy of their maps are judged by the practitioners in terms of the map's correspondence to the reality they perceive and its helpfulness in showing aspects of and relationships among the phenomena that aid them in performing their tasks effectively. Elements in the map are likely to have been obtained from various sources—the way things appeared when they were in school, the ideas of colleagues, the concepts presented in their education courses, and so on. The ones that they retain are usually those that seem to them fairly consistent with the reality they perceive and are useful in guiding their professional activities.

New research is likely to produce new concepts and generalizations or give different emphasis to old ones. Practitioners may hear about them or read about them, but they are not likely to incorporate them into their maps unless they meet one or both criteria—consistency with the reality they perceive, and/or providing guidance for more effective performance of their tasks. The criteria of internal consistency and parsimonious explanation, which are important to researchers, appear to have little significance to the practitioner, and this is often the reason why some research reports are given little attention by practitioners and evoke no changes in their behavior.

USES OF DEVELOPMENT

Most teachers recognize that they use many systems and products developed by others. I have asked groups of teachers, "How did you come to adopt this instructional system?" Two answers predominate. They are employing a system with which they became familiar in their professional preparation, or it is the system which was in use in the school when they began working there. There are two other answers less frequently given. The system was adopted because what they were using earlier was not satisfactory, or the system was adopted because of pressure from parents, the administration, or other "outside forces." The adoption of phonic approaches in reading and the "new math" are illustrations of the latter.

Much more frequently than the adoption of a new system by a teacher is the adoption of a part that can be integrated with the system previously in use. This was reported to occur when teachers recognized that the new part could help achieve a desired objective or could relieve them of an activity which they found distasteful or boring. The use of computer-assisted instruction for drill and practice in mathematics, of audio cassettes in spelling drill and, of course, workbooks, are common examples of the adoption of part of a system to relieve the teacher of onorous tasks.

I have found five common criticisms by teachers of new products or systems:

1. "It takes a good deal of practice before you can make it work."
2. "It is hard to manage."
3. "Most of my students do about as well without using it."
4. "It is too mechanical and takes the challenge out of teaching."
5. "It is too expensive."

The first two are the most frequently voiced criticisms, which suggests that developers give too little attention to the problems practitioners face in using something new. If they consider themselves good teachers, they are faced with the possible loss of this reputation if they handle a seemingly complex new system or product ineptly. This consideration may cause them to resist the adoption of the new system.

When teachers, individually or collectively, select a new system or product, a chief criterion is the ease of using it. Totally new systems are rarely selected, and products are preferred that fit into the old system and do not require much training in their use. However, one barrier to the adoption of otherwise attractive systems is the use of the term "teacher-proof" or "administrator-proof" that was applied several years ago to certain products of development. This term is offensive to practitioners and turns them away from use of these products. It arouses resentment not only because practitioners do not wish to believe that their work can be done by a machine but, more importantly, they know that teaching and administration are human enterprises. They may be assisted by machines, but they cannot be replaced by them. Practitioners know that their students' motivation to learn what the school seeks to teach, the encouragement their students get to try the learning task, and the satisfactions they obtain from succeeding in their learning are all developed in a social context and, particularly with children, in the context of the school which is largely stimulated by the staff.

The failure of developers to understand the importance of the social influence and social context of learning is well illustrated by the effort some years ago to develop and market courses that were solely or primarily composed of programmed learning materials. Persons, particularly young people, became restless and bored with a sequential series of activities, most of which were solitary in nature. For example, a child will practice alone throwing the ball at the basket to improve his skill, but only as this is interspersed with playing the game of basketball. The child's motivation is developed and maintained by his interest in playing basketball, not by developing a skill in isolation. This suggests the conditions and the limits of the usefulness of solitary learning activities, and they need to be understood and elaborated by those working on development.

INNOVATION AS A RESPONSE TO RECOGNIZED PROBLEMS

It has long been noted that practitioners use new systems or new materials most often when they believe that these innovations will help them in dealing with problems that they recognize. For example, multilevel reading collections are widely utilized because these materials enable all the children in the class to read about the same topic in spite of the wide variations in the reading skills among the pupils. Using these materials, teachers can continue to employ their usual group instructional procedure without great modification and still provide for some of the individual differences within their classes.

Most teachers do not believe that their school requires revolutionary reforms to be effective. They know that the majority of their students learn what the parents and the community believe to be the important outcomes of schooling. Reports of the National Assessment of Educational Progress, for example, show that about 90 percent of 17-year-olds can add, subtract, multiply and divide with whole numbers, and about 80 percent can read and comprehend the common reading materials in our society—newspapers, directions for the use of commodities and appliances, and the like, and materials employing simple vocabulary, without complex syntax. Schools in which most children learn what is expected of them are not likely to seek new systems and devices, except those that assist in certain difficulties they have encountered or certain tasks which are boring or distasteful to the teacher or administrator.

There are, however, serious problems in certain fields or in certain places where the school is ready to adopt developments that appear likely to alleviate, if not solve, the problems that are recognized. The education of disadvantaged children is an illustration. Schools with a considerable concentration of children from families with limited education and income commonly recognize the fact that these children are not learning what the school tries to teach. Several systems designed to help disadvantaged children with the learning of reading and arithmetic are employed in many of these schools. Citizenship education is another example where schools are recognizing problems and are looking for new systems to help. In general, innovations are likely to be sought by schools that recognize serious problems they are encountering. If they find systems and products that appear to furnish help in dealing with these problems, the innovations are likely to be given careful consideration and will be adopted if they appear to be manageable and not costly.

MIDDLEMEN IN RESEARCH AND DEVELOPMENT

In the past, few researchers have worked directly with large numbers of practitioners. Teacher training institutions and vendors, particularly textbook publishers and distributors, have served as middlemen. Certain new concepts and principles derived from research become part of the content of education courses, both in preservice and inservice programs, and in this way some of them become part of the cognitive maps of practitioners and guides to their professional thinking and practice. New systems of instruction and management have largely reached practitioners both through education courses and through the demonstrations and teacher guides that commonly accompany the distribution of equipment and materials of instruction. When the results of development are new products, such as equipment and materials for instruction, the extent of their dissemination is largely dependent on the distribution system of vendors.

To a limited extent, state departments of education have served as middlemen in research and development. But their usefulness in this regard has been minor because of other legal responsibilities that have directed their major efforts and because of the traditional attitude of schools that the local district, rather than the state department, bears the chief responsibility for determining what is to be taught and how.

The 1964 Johnson Task Force on Education recognized that the connection between the practitioner and the research and development enterprise had three obvious weaknesses:

1. Much of it was one-way, from researchers and developers to practitioners, rather than two-way, in which the problems and needs of the practitioner were communicated to researchers and developers.
2. It was indirect and informal, depending heavily upon the interests and perceptions of persons who did not view themselves as middlemen.
3. It was slow, often taking several decades for the results of research and development to reach the practitioner.

With these weaknesses in mind, the Task Force recommended the establishment of educational laboratories which would have the responsibility of the middleman function, and would be funded initially by the federal government. On the one hand, the laboratories would work closely with schools and colleges to identify and clarify the problems of practitioners; and, on the other hand, they would be in touch with the research and development enterprise, finding useful concepts, principles, systems, and products that were already in existence and might be adopted and/or adapted by the practitioners in attacking their problems. The laboratories would also stimulate and encourage researchers and developers to work on problems of practitioners on which existent knowledge appeared inadequate to furnish much help.

The legislation authorizing these laboratories was part of Title IV of the Elementary and Secondary Education Act of 1965, and a number of regional laboratories were established. However, few seemed able to develop effective two-way communication and to work closely both with practitioners and those in research and development. Most became research and development centers rather than middlemen, so that today the middleman function is still largely conducted through teacher education institutions and through vendors of educational products.

MAKING EDUCATIONAL RESEARCH AND DEVELOPMENT MORE IMMEDIATELY HELPFUL TO SCHOOLS

Many persons in the research and development enterprise speak and write of their desire to have schools more quickly and fully utilize the results of their work. On the other hand, many practitioners speak of their need for help on their problems—help they believe educational research and development should provide. The foregoing observations on the uses by schools of research and development furnishes some suggestions about things that can be done to make it more immediately helpful to practitioners.

However, an important caveat should be strongly emphasized. Basic research in education should not be expected to be immediately applicable to recognized problems of the practitioner, nor should it be judged or funded in terms of immediate applicability. The purpose of basic research in education is to provide a continually more comprehensive, more accurate, and more unified understanding of the phenomena of education and the conditions and factors influencing it. As our understanding becomes more adequate, practical problems can be dealt with more intelligently and systematically, but the immediate applicability of a piece of basic research cannot and should not be expected.

But studies that seek to derive and to test the implications of basic research concepts and generalizations for educational practices and the development of relevant systems and products can be selected and carried on in ways that furnish more immediate help to the practitioner. The most general suggestion derived from these observations is that persons in research and development who want their work to be employed immediately by the practitioner can be helped greatly by working with practitioners to understand their problems and perceive the context through their eyes.

As an example, I was working not long ago with elementary school teachers who were seeking to improve the learning of disadvantaged children. A program had been designed for this purpose by the curriculum staff in the office of the local board of education. The program was attempted during the previous year without success—the children showed no improvement on tests of reading and arithmetic. In discussing the problem with the teachers, they reported that they could not manage the amount of individualized instruction the program required and they did not understand the principles that seemed to be basic to the program. In an effort to overcome these difficulties, I served as a consultant while they designed a system which seemed to them to be responsive to the problems of their disadvantaged children, and which they believed they could manage. The new program did prove to be one that they learned to conduct and to manage. After three years, the children using the program were making normal progress in reading and arithmetic.

The success of the new curriculum programs developed in the Eight-Year Study can be partly accounted for by the fact that the staff conducting the study served as middlemen between the school practitioners and the research and development enterprise. Throughout the years, and especially in the summer workshops, teachers, administrators and researchers worked together identifying problems, searching for relevant knowledge to attack these problems, and designing systems and preparing materials that were tested in the schools as the project progressed.

In both of these examples—in the development of the program for disadvantaged children and in the Eight-Year Study—serious problems were recognized and the need for help was articulated. When a school recognizes one or more serious problems, the teachers and administrators are likely to be interested in research studies or findings that can help to gain greater understanding of these problems and can suggest ways of attacking them. If the school has a general impression that there are difficulties or problems, it is likely to permit, if not encourage, research directed to the identification of these problems. In such cases, the involvement of members of the school staff in the research activities undertaken has at least two values: (1) the contributions that the school staff can make because of their direct experience with the students, parents, and the community; and (2) the greater use they can make of research ideas and findings with which they have been involved and the implications of which they understand more concretely than just having heard or read reports.

If a school does not recognize a serious problem nor even has a general impression that something is wrong, it is not a promising site for constructive research and development activity. It may change and be a productive place to work at a later time, but until something within the school, or without, stimulates a need for improvement, research and development efforts are likely to encounter only apathy or resistance.

When persons from the research and development enterprise work with practitioners, they need to recognize that the context of the school is likely to be perceived by the practitioner differently than by many researchers and developers. For example, researchers and developers often have a conception of the teacher's activities as similar to those of the ideal physician, diagnosing and treating individuals. Most teachers, however, view their work as group teaching, where the teacher's role is more like that of the general dietitian who plans the menus to furnish a proper balance among proteins, carbohydrates, fats, minerals, and other essential nutrients. Most people eat a healthy diet when it is available, especially if the atmosphere of the eating establishment and the suggestions on the menu are supportive. And most students learn when the home and community have inculcated desirable goals, the school provides a supportive environment, and the teacher has developed a "nutritious program" that he or she manages encouragingly and with zest. As most individuals are able, without diagnosis, to care for their individual differences in nutrition, so most students are able to care for many of their individual differences in learning without specific individual diagnosis.

The latter view is often held unconsciously by teachers, growing out of their experience. It is not usually a result of their program of teacher education. In several typical preservice courses for teachers, the instructional task is described as an individual one, involving diagnosis and prescription but as teachers encounter the usual working situation, they do not see how to manage this kind of individualization with 30 or more children in their classes. Soon, they adopt the common practice of group teaching. This needs to be understood if those in research and development are to help teachers with their tasks. Where possible, this could mean research and development that would improve individualization in group contexts. Where this appears not to be possible, research and development will need to work out a new organization and utilization of staff to deal with significant problems in the individualization of school learning. I mention this difference in the conception of teaching between some research and development persons and some teachers only as an illustration of the need for researchers and developers to understand the context of the school and the role of the teacher as perceived by the practitioner; this understanding is important if research and development activities are to be made more immediately useful to the practitioner.

Conversely, as practitioners work with persons in the research and development enterprise, they should be helped to see more clearly what kinds of knowledge, systems, and products can be furnished by the research and development effort. This should help to prevent impossible expectations on the one hand, or disillusionment and cynicism on the other.

In summary, some of the results of research and development are now employed in the schools, but the process of transmission is indirect, spotty, and slow. The process can be improved by focusing applied research and development on serious problems encountered by schools, by encouraging cooperative attacks on problems in which both research and development personnel and practitioners are involved, and by delineating the roles of middlemen more clearly and encouraging their activities. Above all, there needs to be a fuller comprehension of the kinds of contributions to practice that research and development are capable of making.

REFERENCES

Dewey, J. *Interest and effort in education.* Clifton, N. J.: Augustus M. Kelley Publishers, 1913.

Author Index

Italicized page numbers designate pages on which complete references are given.

B

Barnard, C., 40, *43*
Barth, R. S., 37, *43*
Berlyne, D. E., 36, *43*
Block, J. H., 74, *81*
Bloom, B. S., 70, 74, *81*
Brazelton, T. B., 57, *65*
Bridges, E. M., 41, *43*
Bronson, G., 57, *64*

C

Caldwell, B. M., 56, 57, 60, *64*
Campbell, A., 15, *18*
Campbell, R. F., 39, 40, 41, *43, 44*
Carlisle, D. H., 89, *91*
Carroll, J. B., 69, *81*
Chandrasekhar, S., 31, *43*
Chase, F. S., 8, *18*
Clark, D. L., 17, *18*
Colvin, S. S., 30, *43*
Comber, L. C., 69, *81*
Cone, P. E., 89, *91*
Converse, P. E., 15, *18*
Cooley, W. W., 88, *91*
Corbally, J. E., 41, *43*

Cremin, L., 33, *43*
Cronbach, L. J., 28, *43*
Cubberley, E. P., 38, *43*

D

Dewey, J., 34, 42, *43,* 94, *105*
Dickson, W. J., 39, *44*

E

Ehrhardt, A. E., 56, *65*
Erikson, E. H., 50, 51, *64*

F

Farnen, R. F., 70, *82*
Foshay, A. W., 70, *81*

G

Getzels, J. W., 37, 39, 40, *43, 44*
Glaser, R., 87, 88, *91*
Grusec, J. E., 52, 53, *65*
Guba, E. G., 40, *43*

107